$13 3/2

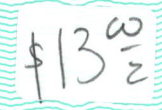

**BETA TESTING
THE ONGOING
APOCALYPSE**

Also by Tom Kaczynski:

TRANS TERRA (FORTHCOMING)
CARTOON DIALECTICS (ONGOING)

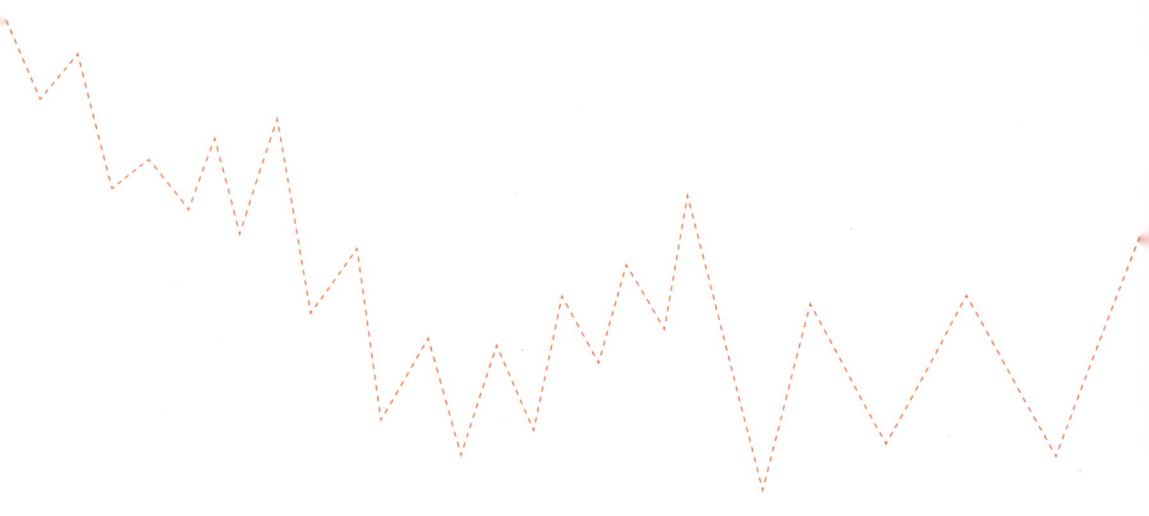

BETA TESTING THE ONGOING APOCALYPSE

By Tom Kaczynski

Editor: Eric Reynolds
Design by Tom Kaczynski
Additional Production by Paul Baresh
VP / Associate Publisher: Eric Reynolds
Published by Gary Groth

Fantagraphics Books, Inc.
7563 Lake City Way NE
Seattle WA 98115 USA
fantagraphics.com

Beta Testing the Ongoing Apocalypse is copyright © 2022 Tom Kaczynski.
This edition © 2022 Fantagraphics Books, Inc. All rights reserved.
Permission to reproduce material from this book, except for purposes
of review and/or notice, must be obtained by the publisher or author.

First printing: January 2022

ISBN 978-1-68396-431-5

Printed in China

FOR NIKKI

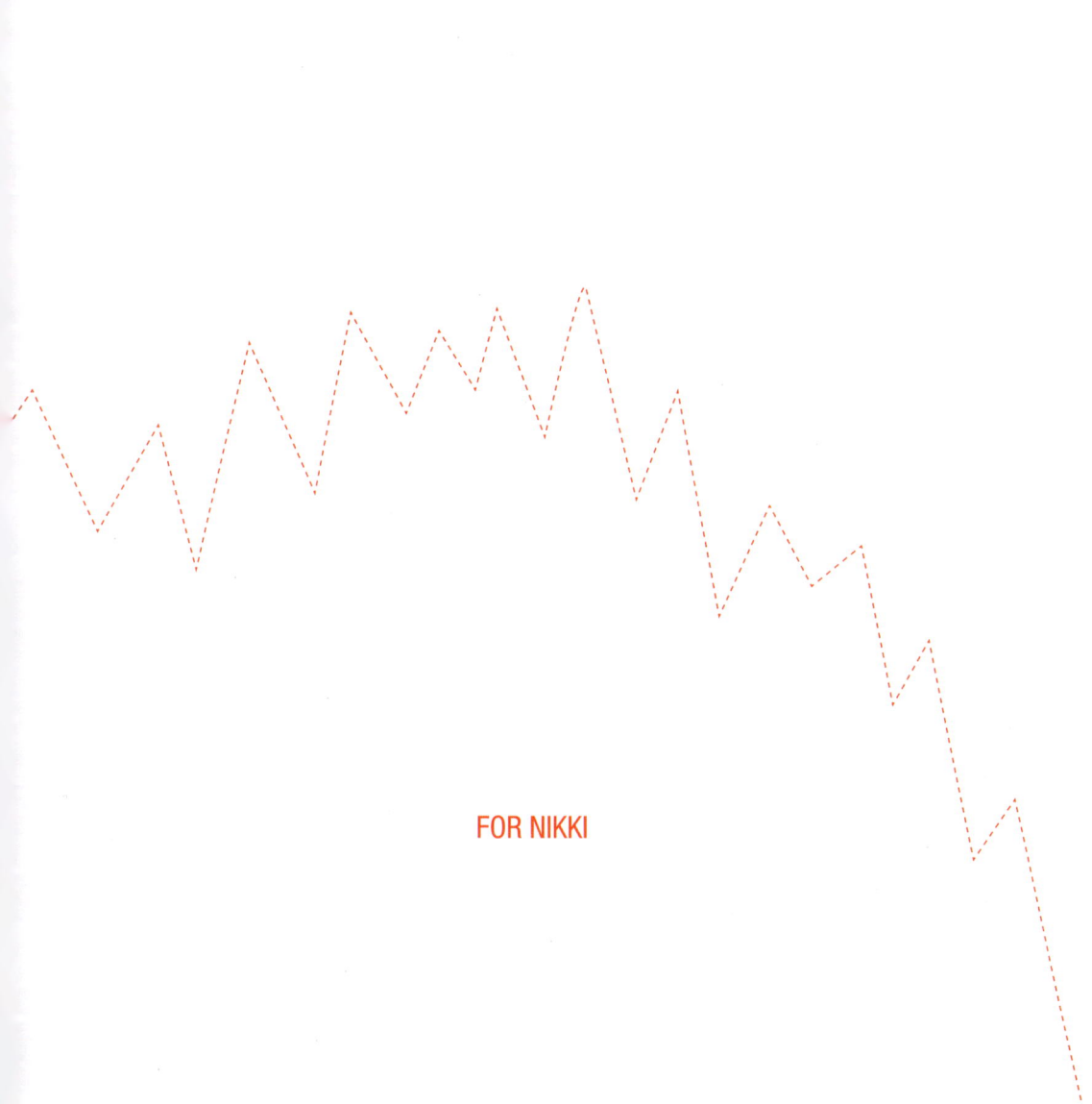

SPACE

100,000 MILES

10,000 Miles

1,000 Miles

100 Miles

1 Mile

BETA TESTING THE ONGOING APOCALYPSE

BY TOM KACZYNSKI

TABLE OF CONTENTS

AND APPROXIMATE SPACE-TIME TRAJECTORIES OF THE NARRATIVES AS MEASURED FROM: MINNEAPOLIS, MN, USA IN 2012-2021 AD

rulers are not to scale

P. VI INTRODUCTION BY CHRISTOPHER BROWN

P. 170 NOTES AND THEORIES

P. 182 INDEX

P. 160 U

P. 46 PH

1,000,000,000 BC   1,000,000 BC   500,000 BC   40,000

P. 45 **WHITE NOISE**

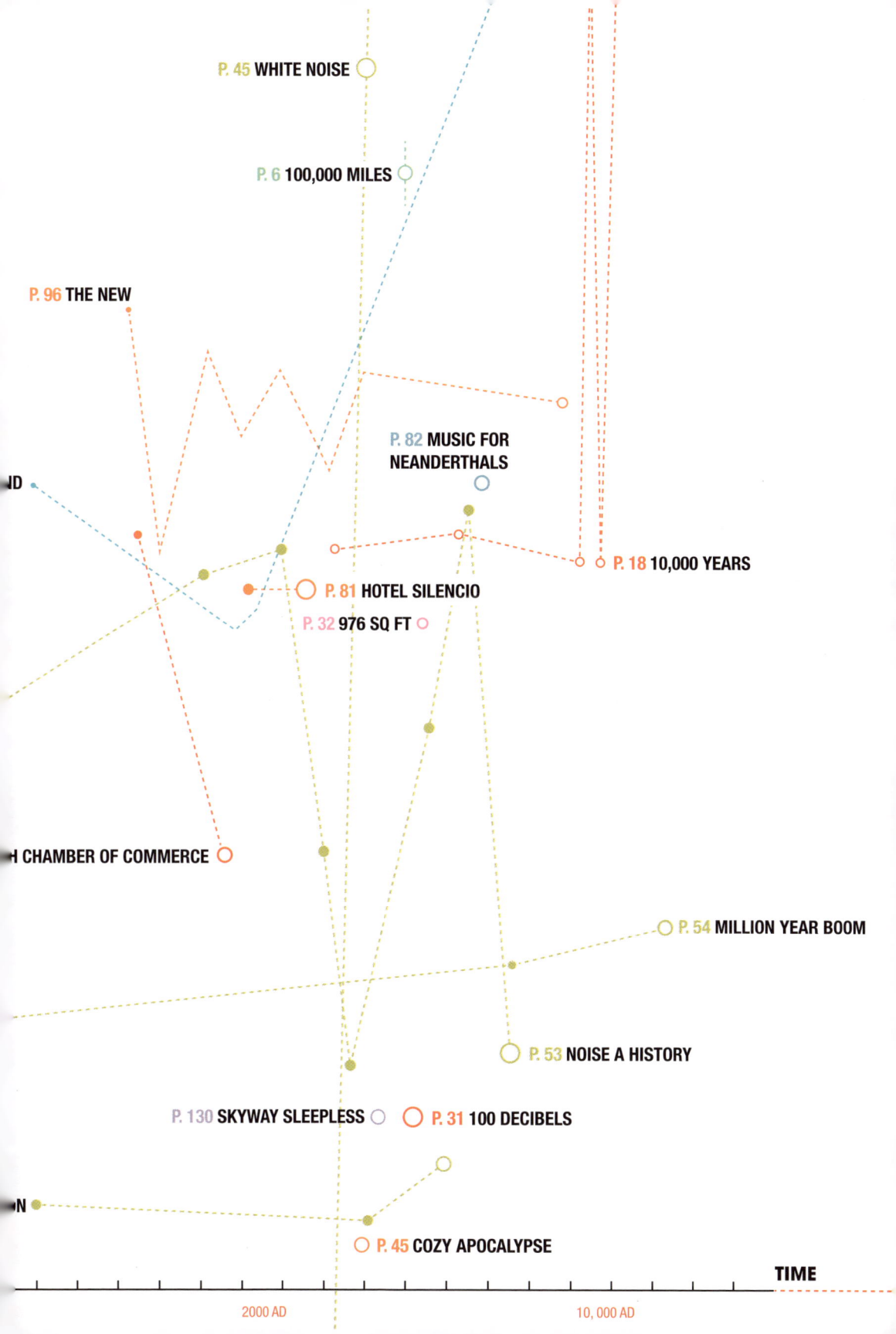

P. 6 **100,000 MILES**

P. 96 **THE NEW**

P. 82 **MUSIC FOR NEANDERTHALS**

P. 18 **10,000 YEARS**

P. 81 **HOTEL SILENCIO**

P. 32 **976 SQ FT**

CHAMBER OF COMMERCE

P. 54 **MILLION YEAR BOOM**

P. 53 **NOISE A HISTORY**

P. 130 **SKYWAY SLEEPLESS**   P. 31 **100 DECIBELS**

P. 45 **COZY APOCALYPSE**

TIME

2000 AD   10,000 AD

THE FACE ON MARS NODS IN SILENT APPROVAL

AN INTRODUCTION
BY CHRISTOPHER BROWN

I first encountered the work of Tom Kaczynski through a doorway decorated with a 1970s painting of a unicorn, on the shelves of Austin's oldest and best comics shop, in one of the early issues of *Mome*, Fantagraphics' pioneering take on the literary magazine. There was a ton of amazing work in there by diverse artists, but Tom K's stood out to me, as if I had discovered the J. G. Ballard of sequential art—someone who was repurposing a popular and often juvenile form into a laboratory of big ideas and radical critique powered by innovative storytelling.

Rereading those stories now, across what feels like just a few years but spans the Global War on Terror, international financial meltdown, the smartphone + social media Singularity, a crippling global pandemic, and the tribalized see-saw of four American presidencies, I see how much more is going on—not just in how well the stories hold up, somehow seeming fresher than when they were new, revealing an oracular prescience in what seemed at the time more like a smarter variation on ironic Clowesian insight. I'm tempted to say Tom Kaczynski is the three-panel Tarkovsky, but that doesn't give the creator of these stories enough credit for his singular artistic vision, or the big-hearted feeling that charges them.

A specter is haunting these stories—the dream of utopia, and the reckoning with its impossibility. These are comics infused with a humanism that channels the deep history of our species, helping us understand how our alienated stumblings through the skywalks, shopping malls and office corridors of contemporary American life are rooted in our natures as naked apes who mastered fire and language and the ability to imagine worlds we can never fully make real.

"When I was young," remarks the narrator of "Phase Transition," a seemingly simple four-page vignette about a guy getting up from his TV to go walk outside, "I imagined the grain silos to be artifacts from some antediluvian civilization." It's a great line, conjuring sublime wonder from a boring Midwestern landscape. But as you read on, following the guy as he walks in there and has a run-in with a stray dog—an animal that has escaped our domestication, and reintroduced feral danger into the sanitized cityscape—you realize just how much that framing reveals the deep truth. The grain silos are temples to the accumulation of surplus, expressions of the trajectory of human civilization since the dawn of agriculture and with it, the invention of cities and math and the written word. They express a power almost beyond our imagining, but they also embody the tragedy of how, in our mastery of nature to serve us, we obliterate our connection to our own wilder natures, and our ability to ever be authentically free.

Tom Kaczynski lets you feel that and see it in a few panels of cartooning, and makes you laugh along the way, taking the narrative rule of "show, don't tell" to new levels.

"Billions served, zero satisfied." In "100,000 Miles," the oldest of these stories, Kaczynski unpacks a Borgesian atlas of life in the post-industrial city from no more than the universal experience of driving to work in rush hour traffic. The core ideas that power all of these stories are there in the first one, and so is the narrative innovation. Each successive panel delivers a new idea through keen observation, while at the same time dialing up the feeling in equal measure. These are not essays, or history lessons, or theory toons—they are deeply human stories. But they are unafraid to disregard all the usual truisms about how such stories are supposed to work.

The characters in these stories don't really change, not in the way writing coaches would have us believe they have to. They find themselves, by learning to see. Tom K's characters have revelations about how the world around them really works, about what's really going on at the office, about what their own true natures are. They realize the deep lie at the heart of the progressive narrative of modern life—that the world never really changes, and the only way to break free from the alienated malaise in which we are trapped is to find ways to express that more authentic self through whatever secret passage out you can find, be it the weedy path below the grain silos, the woods behind the office building, the dream of another planet, or the gutter between the panels.

"Fuck it let's build a Ziggurat," says one of the characters attending a party in "Utopia Dividend," the newest of the pieces added for this updated edition of the collection. The story deploys Kaczynski's unique storytelling gifts in epic mode, following an actor as he travels to a remote private island, where he learns he is being groomed for the corporate colonization of Mars. That beer keg banter reminds us these deep-thoughts-comics don't take themselves too seriously. It also encodes a manifesto we can divine from a collection of cartoons that effortlessly channel Karl Marx and Elon Musk on the same page, remind us what it really feels like to live in this society, and show us the path to our own self-actualization without telling us where to go.

The America of these stories is one we all know, but that only Tom Kaczynski can really see. He brings the singular perspective of one who was raised in Warsaw Pact-era Poland, the son of a Solidarity activist who had to leave the country and its failed dream of socialist utopia for Reagan-era America and its unfulfilled promise of a different kind of utopia. Minnesota, specifically, the Twin Cities, where Northern European immigrants imposed their idea of order on an Ice Age landscape and made room for the Mall of America and a downtown that lets you go to work without ever going outside. These are comics by a design professional who understands the city with the mind of an architect but has the courage to confront how corporate architecture and capitalist infrastructure really make us feel.

Tom Kaczynski is also one of our smartest comics critics, the man who can discover the deeper meaning lurking in the inky heart of our superhero multiverse while also making us laugh our asses off. I would say he is the Donald Judd of the graphic novel, but whereas Judd was the critic who became an artist to prove the points he was making in his writings, Tom K was an artist who expanded his work to share how he reads the comics of others—with his characteristically erudite insights, but never losing the boyish wonder of that kid leaping into the Negative Zone with Reed Richards and his modern family.

Tom Kaczynski is also one of those rare artists who seems to spend more time helping out his colleagues than promoting his own work, as a publisher and teacher in addition to his writing on the field. That generosity is the other thing that makes this republication and expansion of his Eisner Award-nominated collection such a wonderful thing, especially for those of us who have admired his work since his earliest appearances. In those days he signed his comics as Tom K. Reading this work now, you may join me in realizing it's time to learn how to properly say Kaczynski (hint: it sounds a lot like Ka-Ching!), because it's one of those names you are going to be citing in the future.

Christopher Brown is the Philip K. Dick, Campbell, and World Fantasy Award-nominated author of *Tropic of Kansas*, *Rule of Capture*, and *Failed State*.

SPACE

— 100,000 MILES

— 10,000 Miles

C 45
M 0
Y 100
K 0

100,000 MILES

Originally appeared in *Backwards City Review*, 2006
First appearance in color: *MOME 7*, 2007

— 1,000 Miles

— 100 Miles

— 1 Mile

1,000,000,000 BC — 1,000,000 BC — 500,000 BC — 40,000 BC

2000 AD   10,000 AD   **TIME**

100,000 MILES...

THE STARTING POINT IS ARBITRARY. FROM THERE, THE CITY EXPANDS IN ALL DIRECTIONS AT THE SPEED OF A CAR.

THE SUM TOTAL OF ALL THE CARS' ODOMETERS IS THE MEASURE OF ITS SUCCESS: PURE ACCUMULATION OF DISTANCE.

ITS INHABITANTS PREFER TO EXPERIENCE IT AT 75 MPH. THE CONSTANT SPEED AND MOTION IS NOT WITHOUT INCIDENT.

HOLY SHIT!

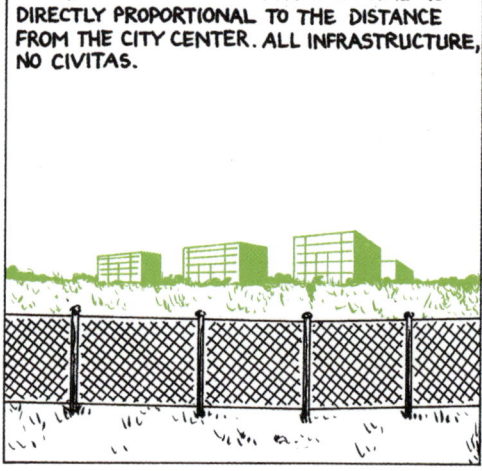

THE CRASH IS A VIOLENT CONTRACTION OF SPACE, A SUDDEN COLLAPSE OF THE CITY IN MINIATURE.	

THE VEHICLE, LIKE A MECHANICAL PROCRUSTES, TRANSFORMS ITS PASSENGERS INTO ABSTRACT PORTRAITS OF THE CITY.	THE CRASH REVEALS THE HIDDEN LOGIC OF THE MORNING COMMUTE, THE TRIP TO THE MALL, THE PLEASURE DRIVE, THE TRAFFIC JAM.

"GOTTA GET AN SUV..."

EVERY WEEKDAY THE PEOPLE ENDURE GREAT DISTANCES TO REACH THEIR PLACES OF WORK.	THE AMBITION TO ACCUMULATE CAPITAL IS DIRECTLY PROPORTIONAL TO THE DISTANCE FROM THE CITY CENTER. ALL INFRASTRUCTURE, NO CIVITAS.

Versailles Office Park
Next Exit

EACH COMPLEX IS A SCALE MODEL OF SOME FUTURE MEGALOPOLIS. A CORPORATE UTOPIA. THE CITY AS A GLOBAL CONSTELLATION OF FINANCIAL TRANSACTIONS.

SUBMERGED WITHIN THE VIRTUAL REALITY OF ETERNAL GROWTH ECONOMICS, THE WORKERS MISS THE SIGNIFICANCE OF THEIR LOCATION.

...BAD TRAFFIC

EXPLAIN LATENESS!

THE CAR IS AN INCUBATOR.

UGH WORK...

IT'S A SKINNER BOX, A PSYCHOLOGICAL EXPERIMENT, A DEPRIVATION CHAMBER.

THE STEERING WHEEL, THE INSTRUMENT PANEL, THE ACCELERATION PEDAL, THEY ALL NURTURE THE ILLUSION OF CONTROL AND INDEPENDENCE.

BEHIND THE WHEEL, EACH CITIZEN OF THE CITY MUTATES INTO AN INDIVIDUAL. A SELF-MADE MAN WITHOUT DEBT TO ANYONE OR ANYTHING.

WORK CAN WAIT!

THE ROAD AS LIFE. EACH EXIT AN UNDISCOVERED POSSIBILITY.
Eighth Wonder Shopping Centre
Next 3 Exits
MAYBE I SHOULD CHECK OUT NEW GADGETS AT THE MALL?
TOY
THE CONDITIONING BEGINS EARLY. THE MEMORIES OF THE CITY ARE CAR MEMORIES.
MORE THAN MEETS THE EYE!
THE CAR AND DESIRE BECOME LOCKED IN A CARNAL EMBRACE BEHIND THE WINDOWS OF A SUBURBAN VAN.
CLIMAXING IN AN AIR-CONDITIONED ORGY OF CONSUMPTION. BILLIONS SERVED, ZERO SATISFIED.

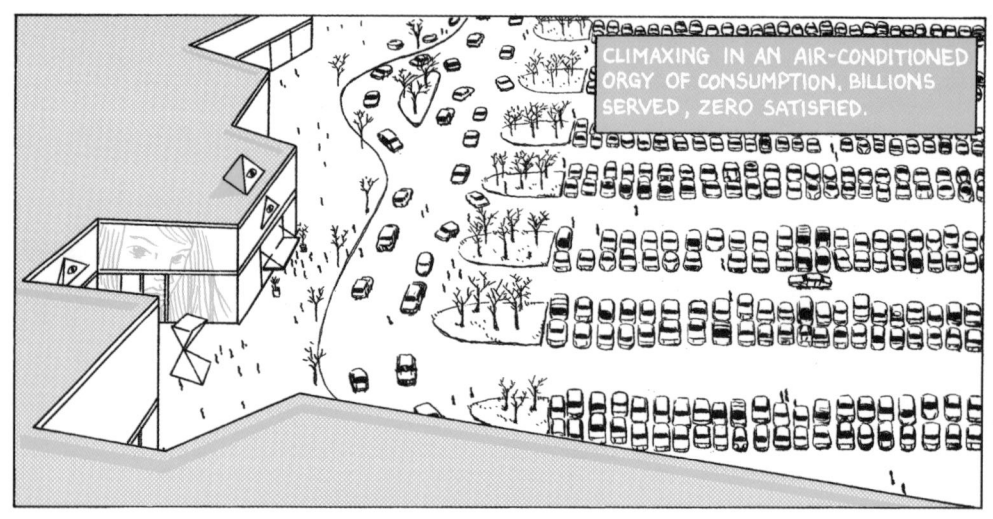

CAUGHT ON A NEVERENDING HEDONIC TREADMILL, THE INHABITANTS SEEK MORE STABLE GROUND.

NOSTALGIA FOR WALKING STIRS THEIR ATROPHIED LIMBS. LONG DORMANT MUSCLE MEMORY STEERS THEM DOWNTOWN.

THIS WAS ONCE THE TRADITIONAL CENTER TEEMING WITH INTENSE HUMAN ACTIVITY UNMEDIATED BY THE GLASS OF A WINDSHIELD.

BUT THE CENTER IS A VOID, AN EMPTY SHELL.

THE DOWNTOWN SURVIVES AS A HOLLOW CORE. ITS SPATIAL QUALITY DEPLETED BY A NEGATIVE ARCHITECTURE.

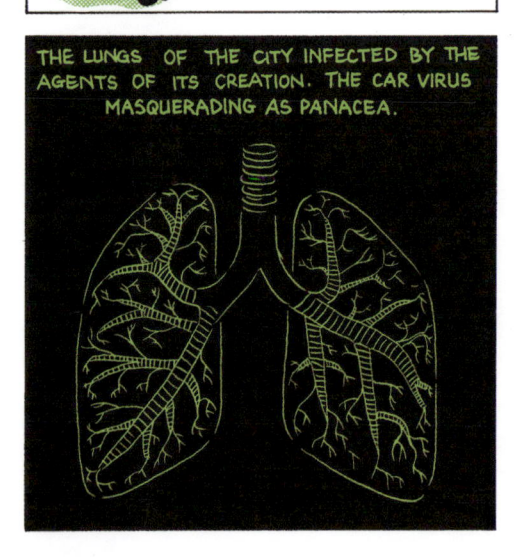

THE WEAKENED CENTER OPENED PROMISING NEW VISTAS.	THE SUBURBAN HOUSE WAS SUPPOSED TO BE A BUCOLIC RETREAT; A PLACE FREE FROM TOXIC CIVILIZATION; A BREATH OF FRESH AIR.
A COLLECTIVE WILL TO SUBURBIA MANIFESTED IN PRE-FAB, RUSTIC, ANTI-URBAN ENCLAVES.	CUL-DE-SAC BLOOMS SPREAD EVERYWHERE. EACH DEAD END A DESPERATE ATTEMPT TO CONCEAL THE EXTENT OF ITS SELF-DELUSION.
THE LUNGS OF THE CITY INFECTED BY THE AGENTS OF ITS CREATION. THE CAR VIRUS MASQUERADING AS PANACEA.	IN THIS CITY, EVERYONE HAS A TERMINAL CONDITION.

THE INHABITANTS ARE FOREVER TRAPPED IN AN ENDLESS LABYRINTH OF ASPHALT MOBIUS STRIPS.
HERE'S THE WORK EXIT AGAIN---
IT'S A THIN, VISCOUS MEMBRANE OF REPETITIVE ODOMETRIC ACTIVITY. WORK. DRIVE. SHOP. DRIVE. CRASH. REPEAT.
I SUPPOSE I SHOULD GO--- SIGH---
RZ6COM
WHOA! IS THIS WHAT I SAW EARLIER?
THE BURNED OUT HUSKS ON THE SIDE OF THE ROAD ARE A REFLECTION OF THE CITY'S SPATIAL DISCONTINUITY, A MIRROR REALITY RESEMBLING OUR OWN.
37ZEL
TRAFFIC SLOWS TO A CRAWL, EACH CAR PAYING A 5 MPH TRIBUTE, A SILENT RECOGNITION OF THE TWISTED BLUEPRINT OF AN UNCERTAIN FUTURE.
ESSO

THE TRAFFIC JAM IS AN ONTOLOGICAL DISRUPTION. THE SLOW MOTION BOREDOM TRANSFORMS THE CAR INTO A USELESS STEEL BOX.
THE HUMANS BECOME AGITATED, NERVOUS. SUBCONSCIOUS FEARS SURFACE. WILL IT EVER MOVE AGAIN?
A NEW ESCHATOLOGY EMERGES. IS THIS IT? THE FINAL TRAFFIC JAM? 100,000 MILES OF CARS IN SUSPENDED ANIMATION. SOMEWHERE AHEAD, ONE BY ONE, EACH VEHICLE IS BEING DISASSEMBLED AND DECONSTRUCTED TO MAKE ROOM FOR A NEW REALITY.
THE DISORIENTED DRIVERS ARE LEFT TO WANDER ON FOOT. THE HIDDEN ARCHITECTURE OF THE CITY REVEALED TO THEM AMONG THE PILLARS OF ABANDONED OVERPASSES.
THE END

SPACE

— 100,000 MILES

— 10,000 Miles

C 0
M 80
Y 80
K 0

10,000 YEARS

First appearance: *MOME 8*, 2007

— 1,000 Miles

— 100 Miles

— 1 Mile

1,000,000,000 BC   1,000,000 BC   500,000 BC   40,000 B

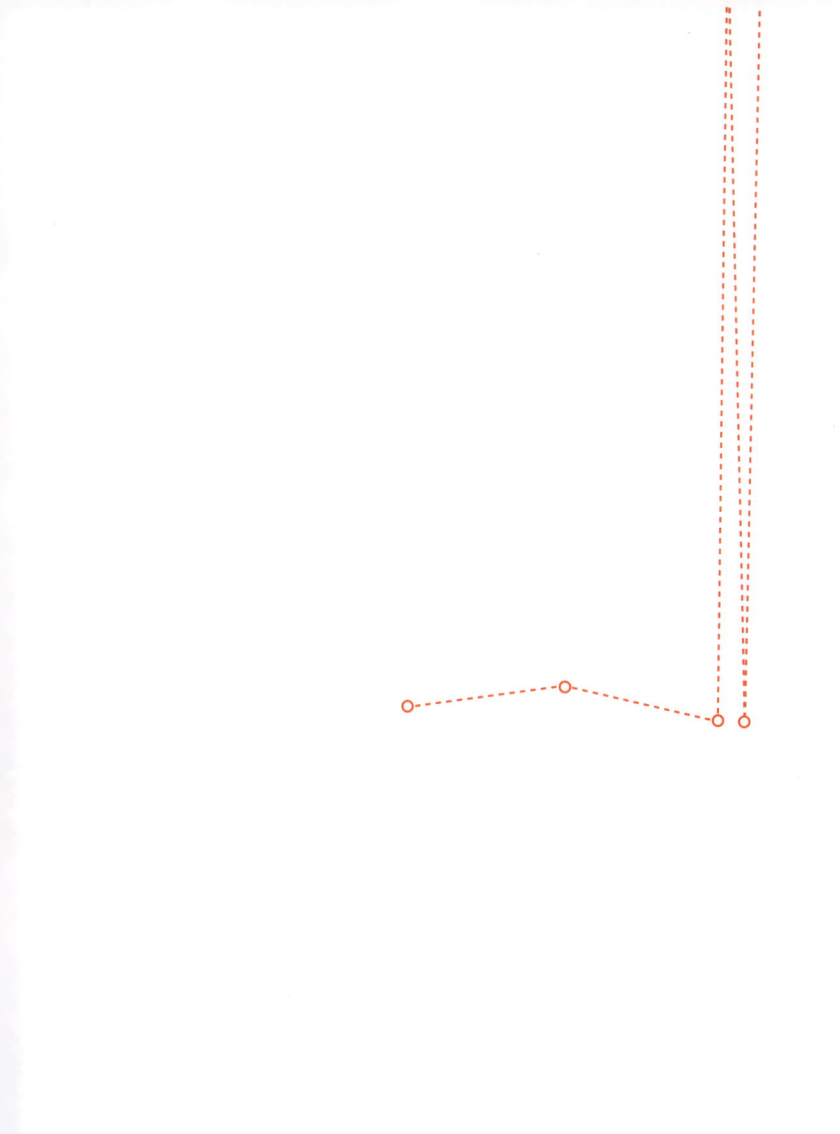

2000 AD   10,000 AD   **TIME**

PLEASE, MISTER CAYCE, CONTINUE.
I DON'T KNOW WHAT I WAS DOING IN MADAME KATHERINE ŽIŽMOR'S OFFICE. I NEVER CONSIDERED MYSELF A SUBJECT WORTHY OF PSYCHIC THERAPY.
I WALKED IN WITHOUT AN APPOINTMENT, COMPELLED BY SOME OCCULT FORCE TO CONSULT THIS UNLIKELY ORACLE.
YOUR FREE PREDICTION: BUY SPACE STOCKS.
IF ONLY THE DJ HADN'T SWITCHED TO THE RADIO BRIEFLY A FEW WEEKS AGO...
...NEW CLUES REVEAL THE POSSIBILITY OF LIFE ON MARS...
?
PSHHH
IF, ON MY WAY HOME I HADN'T LOOKED UP... I MAY NOT HAVE NOTICED HER.
HMM, IS IT CARBON BASED OR WHAT?
THE AD WAS RIDICULOUS, LIKE A PITCH FOR CHEAP ACNE TREATMENT, OR A THIRD RATE TECHNICAL COLLEGE. BUT ITS ABSURDITY ILLUMINATED OUR TENUOUS CONNECTION.
FEEL LIKE A MARTIAN?
▲ Psychic Therapy
▲ Akashic Records Search
▲ Interpretation of Dreams
Madame Žiźmor PHD
I HAD A DREAM. SHE INTERPRETED DREAMS. IT WAS ENOUGH FOR ME. I HAD TO SEE HER.
I OPENED MY EYES...

I FELT REBORN... OR RATHER I FELT THE WORLD WAS REBORN AROUND ME...
I WAS WEAK AT FIRST. I COULD ONLY CONSUME LIQUIDS.
I REGAINED STRENGTH RAPIDLY. AND STARTED CRAVING SOLIDS.
THE HOSPITAL PSYCHOLOGIST TOLD ME THAT I HAD "SLEPT" FOR TEN THOUSAND YEARS.
IT WAS SOME KIND OF TRANCE?
YES.
THE FUTURE WAS A LITTLE DISAPPOINTING. I EXPECTED SOMETHING RADICALLY DIFFERENT, NOT A JOB IN AN ADVERTISING AGENCY.
MANY FAMILIAR PRODUCTS WERE STILL AROUND, BUT WITH EXOTIC NEW FLAVORS.
Lychee Cola
NEW TASTE
Lychee Cola
AS EXPECTED, TECHNOLOGY PROGRESSED. PORTABLE DEVICES WERE MORE POWERFUL AND THINNER THAN EVER BEFORE.
WHO IS THIS?
HOLD
SNAP WRIST
THWIP
READY
THE WORLD WAS FOR SALE AGAIN.
SHOE CITY
SHAPE+ blob
iPILL
INGEST SOUND
NOSTALGIA®
GHOST BEARD
NEW SHAVE
ORO SKY HOMES
AFFORDABLE LUXURY
STRETCH BEAST
ACID WASH
ACID
DETERGENT.
PURE CHOCOLATE LAXATIVE

I GOT AN EXPENSIVE CONDO WITH A BREATHTAKING VIEW, A CUTE GIRLFRIEND (SMART, TOO!)...	...AND A MONOLITHIC TV, WITH MY FAVORITE SHOW: 23RD INTERPLANETARY.

"THE DREAMER IS AWAKE! SUMMON THE LEADER!"

"NEVER CALL ME LEADER! I AM MERELY THE EMERGENT MANIFESTATION OF THE WILL OF OUR COLLECTIVE DISORDER."

THE ACTION TOOK PLACE ON MARS. THERE WAS SOME KIND OF ZOMBIE REVOLUTION UNDERWAY.

"I KNOW. BRING HIM!"

THE DREAMER LOOKED LIKE ME, AT LEAST ACCORDING TO MY BRAND NEW GIRLFRIEND.

"YOU HAVE DREAMED FOR CENTURIES. YOUR DREAMS ARE THE NEW CURRENCY."

"LEADER! WE ARE READY FOR ARMED STRUGGLE!!"

SHEATHE YOUR WEAPONS! LISTEN! A SPECTER IS HAUNTING MARS—THE SPECTRE OF CONSUMERISM. THE STORM OF HISTORY IS APPROACHING. ALL THAT IS SOLID MELTS INTO THE AIR.

CONSUMERS OF THE SOLAR SYSTEM, SAVE YOUR RECEIPTS!

THE END OF THE END OF HISTORY HAS ARRIVED. THE TRAUMA OF THE 20TH CENTURY WILL HEAL. THE PYRAMID CITY WILL WITHER AS WE HAVE WITHERED.

THE SHOPPING CENTERS ARE QUIET AND EMPTY, AWAITING OUR RETURN... AND WE WILL RETURN EVERYTHING!

CAR PARKS AWAIT OUR OCCUPATION. WITHOUT AMPLE PARKING SPACE, CHAOS WILL REIGN IN THE STREETS.

THE OFFICE PYRAMIDS WILL ONCE AGAIN SCREAM WITH THE SILENCE OF TOMBS.

CONSUMER SOCIETY! ACCORDING TO THE LAW OF ETERNAL RETURN, WE DEMAND A REFUND!

WHAT IS THAT INFERNAL NOISE?!

OH...

CHK BEEP BEEP CHK BEEP

MY CELLPHONE RANG AND I MULTI-TASKED INTO SOME OTHER REALITY.

SPARE A CREDIT?

IT'S FOR ME...

BEEP

I DIDN'T KNOW THE NUMBER OF THE CALLER. THE OTHER END OF THE LINE REPLIED WITH RHYTHMIC STATIC LIKE A VACUUM TUBE RADIO TUNED TO THE FREQUENCY OF QUASARS.
HELLO? HELLO? HELLO?
I SEE...
YOUR DREAM OF REVOLUTION, LEADING, PRESUMABLY, TO SOME UTOPIAN DENOUEMENT IS AN INFANTILE CASE OF WISH FULFILLMENT.
UH...
WE ALL DESIRE, BUT CIVILIZATION REQUIRES SACRIFICE. IT CONTROLS OUR MOST BRUTAL AGGRESSIVE AND SEXUAL INSTINCTS. SUBLIME SUBLIMATION.
...ADS DO NOT INTERRUPT AS THEY FILL IN THE BLANKS. THEY FILL THE EMPTINESS OF OUR SOULS. FUNDAMENTALLY WE ARE EMPTY. NATURE ABHORS A VACUUM.
HOW MUCH DO I OWE?
CIVILIZATION SATISFIES DESIRES BY INFLATING THEM. IT'S A TRADE-OFF. SOCIETY CREDITS YOU LIFE AND SECURITY IN EXCHANGE FOR REPRESSION.
CASH? WE PREFER CREDIT, MR CAYCE.
I WAS STILL DREAMING. I DECIDED TO RETURN TO THE CONDO.
DEBT, AND WE'RE ALL BORN WITH IT, IS REPAID WITH ALIENATION...
ZIZMOR
PSYCHIC FREUDIAN ASTROLOGY

I LIVED IN THE CONDOMINIUM DISTRICT. THE ULTRA-MODERN HIGH RISES WERE ERECTED IN A SINGLE WEEKLONG BUILDING ORGY. INSTANT NEIGHBORHOOD.	THE STATE OF THE HALLWAYS REFLECTED THE MOOD OF THE RESIDENTS. I WAS MOVING THROUGH THE CORRIDORS OF SOME KIND OF SLOW MOTION APOCALYPSE.
THE APARTMENT LOOKED MORE 21ST CENTURY THAN BEFORE. ETERNAL SAMENESS PERMEATED ALL OBJECTS. THE FUTURE WAS IN RETREAT.	MY GIRLFRIEND WAS DEAD ASLEEP... OR JUST DEAD...SICK... DEFECTIVE? I COULDN'T BE SURE. I WAS NO LONGER SURE WHAT CENTURY THIS WAS.
I DIDN'T KNOW WHAT TO DO SO I JUST SAT DOWN. TIME FLOWED IN NO PARTICULAR DIRECTION.	I'M NOT SURE AT WHICH MOMENT I NOTICED THAT EVERYTHING WAS AN ELABORATE SET CONSTRUCTED OUT OF PAPIER MÂCHÉ. I WAS SURROUNDED BY HOLLOW EFFIGIES.

HI
I TRIED TO RESIST THE BIOLOGICAL COMPULSION TO EX-CHANGE GENETIC INFORMATION. WE PERFORMED THE TASK MECHANICALLY AND DISPASSIONATELY, LIKE DAMAGED AUTOMATA MIMICKING PORNOGRAPHY.
THE BRIEF MOMENTS POST-ORGASM ARE A STATE OF COMMUNION WITH THE INANIMATE. THE CONSCIOUSNESS WANDERS, ROOTLESS AMONG THE CHEMICAL AND MI-NERAL COMPONENTS OF THE BODY, SEEKING THE MYSTERY OF ITS EXISTENCE.
I TRAVELED IN TIME AGAIN, THIS TIME TO ONE BILLION B.C. IN THE OXYGEN-LESS SKY I SAW A MARTIAN METEOR PENETRATE THE EARTH. THE ORIGIN OF LIFE INFECTED.
SUDDENLY EVOLUTION MAKES SENSE. PROTOPLASMIC CAPITALISM. PROTEIN CURRENCY. AMINO ACID EXCHANGE RATES. MOLECULAR SURPLUS.
FERAL COMPETITION. CARNIVOROUS CONFLICT. REPTILIAN EXPLOITATION. COLD-BLOODED SHOPPING.
PALEOLITHIC CORPORATIONS. CRO-MAG-NON CAPITAL. NEANDERTHAL PROFITS. VIRILE ENTREPRENEURS.

THROUGH THE AEONS, A THIN THREAD OF MARTIAN DNA HAUNTS THE TERRESTRIAL GENOME.
IT'S INSIDE ME. I'M MARTIAN. I DON'T HAVE THE RIGHT CONSTITUTION FOR THIS WORLD. I'M ON THE WRONG PLANET.
WHAT PLANET DO YOU THINK YOU'RE ON, MISTER CAYCE?
THE GROUND SHIFTED. THE PLANETS CHANGED ORBITS. VERTIGO. NAUSEA.
THE ENTIRE SPACE-TIME CONTINUUM BECAME SUSPECT. THE ZODIAC WAS AN ALIEN BESTIARY. CIVILIZATION WAS AN ANCIENT BURIAL GROUND WITH UNFAMILIAR FUNERARY RITES.
MISTER CAYCE
ASTRAL DISASTER.
WE DON'T HAVE A REFUND POLICY...

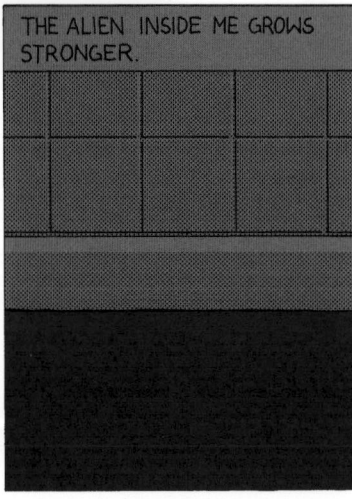

SURPLUS GRAVITY, THE COMPOSITION OF THE ATMOSPHERE, THE ELECTRO-MAGNETIC RADIATION MADE EVERY STEP AN AGONY.	WITH EFFORT I MADE IT UP TO THE APARTMENT.
THE SOUND OF RUNNING WATER SLOWLY DISSOLVED THE MEMORIES OF THE DREAM AND MADAME ŽIŽMOR. *PSSSHH*	THE BUOYANCY OF WATER RELIEVED THE PRESSURE OF GRAVITY. THE WORLD DROWNED IN MY TUB.

BUT MARS REMAINS. I CAN FEEL MY HUMANITY MELT AWAY.	THE ALIEN INSIDE ME GROWS STRONGER.	THE FACE ON MARS NODS IN SILENT APPROVAL.

END

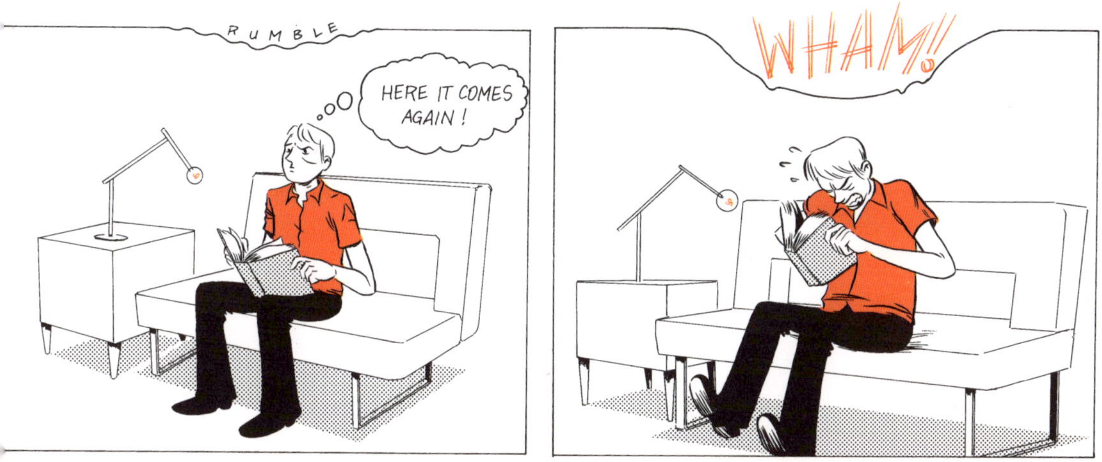
RUMBLE
HERE IT COMES AGAIN!
WHAM!

100 DECIBELS

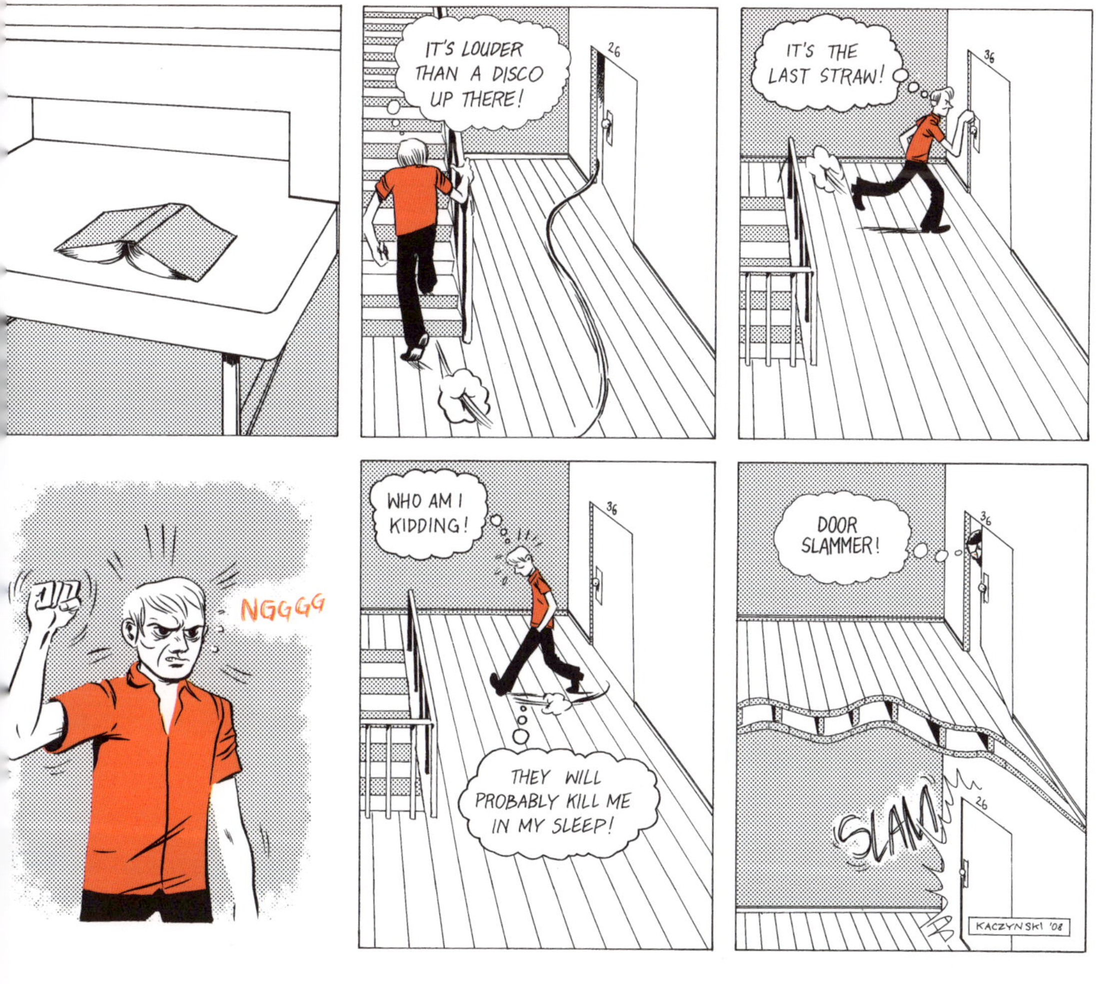
IT'S LOUDER THAN A DISCO UP THERE!
26
IT'S THE LAST STRAW!
36
NGGGG
WHO AM I KIDDING!
36
THEY WILL PROBABLY KILL ME IN MY SLEEP!
DOOR SLAMMER!
36
SLAM
26
KACZYNSKI '08

SPACE

100,000 MILES

10,000 Miles

C 0
M 50
Y 0
K 0

976 SQ. FT.

First appearance: *MOME 9*, 2007

1,000 Miles

100 Miles

1 Mile

1,000,000,000 BC   1,000,000 BC   500,000 BC   40,000

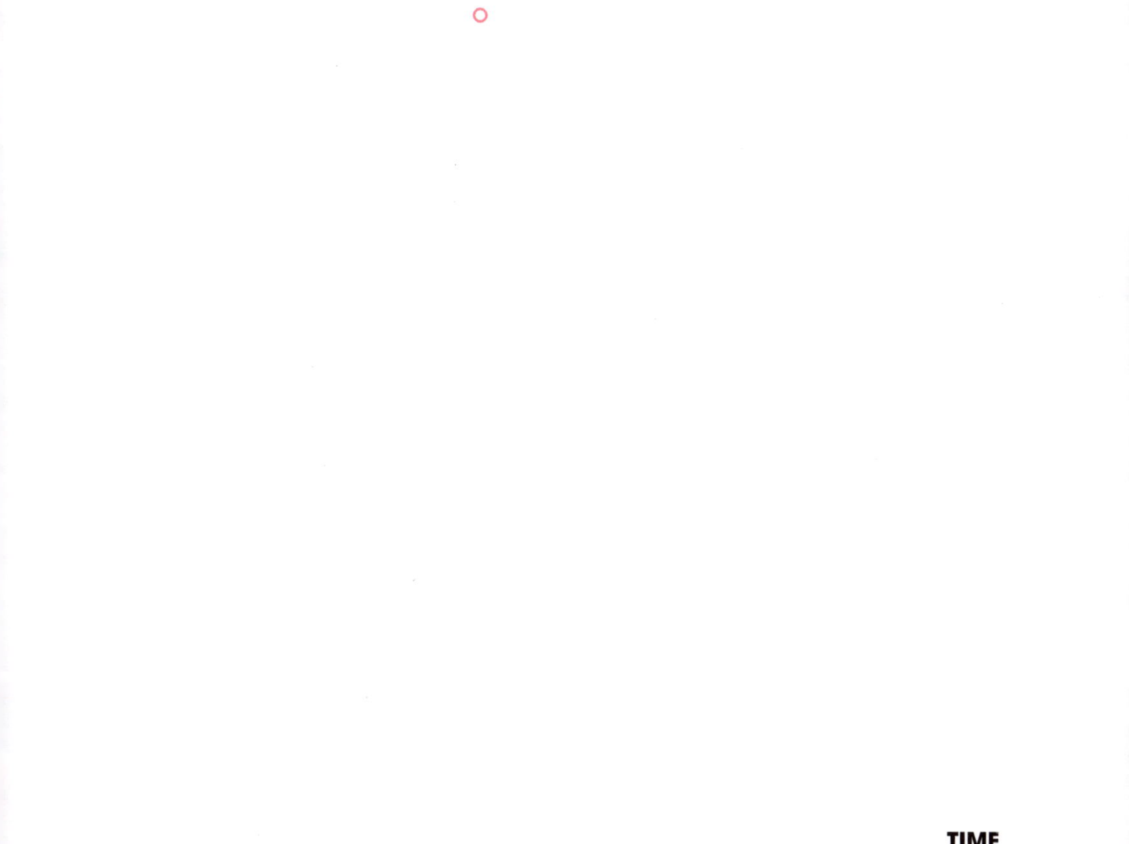

TIME
2000 AD
10, 000 AD

IT'S NADINE.
AND TRIPPY! HE'S SO CUTE! I GUESS HE BELONGS TO ONE OF HER TENANTS.
A FEW MONTHS AGO WE RETURNED TO THE CITY AFTER AN ILL-CONCEIVED ADVENTURE IN SUBURBIA.
HINK ANYONE CAN EE US THROUGH HE SKYLIGHTS?
SHE'S CRAZY, YOU KNOW.
AFTER ENDURING TWO-HOUR COMMUTES AND DRINKING TOO MUCH CORPORATE KOOL-AID, I WAS HAPPY TO BE FREELANCING IN A MAJOR METROPOLIS.
WHO? NADINE?
NO! HER TENANT!
THE NEIGHBORHOOD WE DECIDED TO MOVE INTO WAS A LITTLE ODD...
CRAZY HOW?
...THERE WAS SOMETHING DEFECTIVE ABOUT IT...I COULDN'T HELP BUT TO THINK OF IT AS A CHRONIC PATIENT SUBJECTED TO MULTIPLE UNSUCCESSFUL SURGICAL PROCEDURES.
I DON'T KNOW. SOMETHING TO DO WITH ALIENS...
WHAT D'YOU THINK THAT'S GONNA BE?

ACTUALLY, I HESITATE TO CALL IT A NEIGHBORHOOD. FOUR AND A HALF BLOCKS OF RANDOM BUILDINGS SURROUNDED BY HIGHWAYS, OVERPASSES, A BRIDGE, AND A MAJOR AVENUE HARDLY CONSTITUTES A NEIGHBORHOOD.

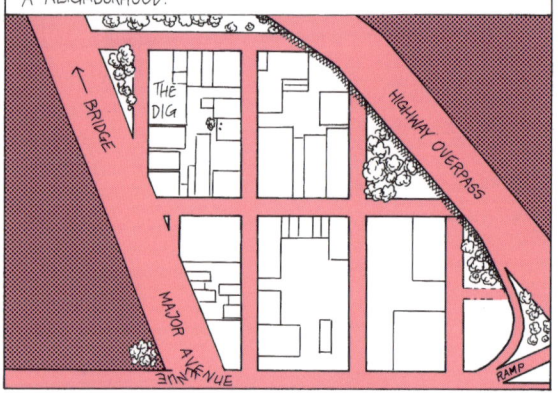

THE AREA'S PROXIMITY TO DOWNTOWN AND A RECENT REAL ESTATE BOOM TRANSFORMED THE CONCRETE BEACHES OF THIS TRAFFIC ISLAND INTO HOT PROPERTY.

A SUBTLE REALITY SHIFT WAS FELT BY ALL RESIDENTS WHEN AN UPSCALE INTERNET GROCER FINALLY DECIDED TO DELIVER TO THE AREA.

MAILBOXES SUDDENLY FILLED WITH JUNK MAIL: CATALOGS OFFERING EXPENSIVE FURNITURE, SAMPLES OF HIGH END COSMETICS, AND COUPONS FOR TRENDY DAY SPAS.

THE NEIGHBORHOOD STARTED TO REGISTER AS A BLIP ON THE DEMOGRAPHIC RADAR.

LUXURY IN THE HEART OF RAMBO
HIVIEWTOWERS.COM

I GUESS WE NOW LIVE SOMEPLACE CALLED RAMBO!

A FEW MONTHS LATER I BEGAN HEARING AN UNUSUAL NOISE AT NIGHT. IT DIDN'T HAPPEN EVERY NIGHT, BUT IT RETURNED RELATIVELY FREQUENTLY.
SHHHKHHHH
SHHKHHHHH
IT SOUNDED EXACTLY LIKE THE SCRAPING SOUND A SHOVEL MAKES WHILE DIGGING. I WAS PARALYZED WITH FEAR. WHO WAS DIGGING IN THE MIDDLE OF THE NIGHT? I DIDN'T WANT TO KNOW!
SHHHKHHHHH
EVENTUALLY, INSOMNIA AND CURIOSITY OVERCAME MY PARANOIA AND I CHANCED A PEEK AT THE BACK YARD.
SHHHKHHHH
SHHKHHHH
IT TURNED OUT TO BE NOTHING BUT TATTERED, PLASTIC INSULATION FLAPPING IN THE WIND. THE UNFINISHED CONDO FIRED THE FIRST SHOT IN ITS PSYCHOLOGICAL WARFARE WITH THE NEIGHBORHOOD.
SHHHKHHH
SHHHKHHHH
UGH... I HAD THIS HORRID NIGHTMARE...
YEAH?
I'M TRAPPED IN THIS TINY PADDED SPACE. IT'S SORT OF LIKE THE INSIDE OF A COFFIN... AND THERE IS THIS MUTED SOUND OF SHOVELING... LIKE I'M BEING BURIED ALIVE... AND I CAN'T GET OUT...
SHHKHHH
BAH! IT'S THAT STUPID CONDO! THE INSULATION MAKES A WEIRD DIGGING SOUND IN THE WIND!
HOW STRANGE...
IT'S AFFECTING YOUR DREAMS!

AS THE CONDO GREW, SO DID ITS GRIP ON THE COLLECTIVE IMAGINATION OF THE NEIGHBORHOOD. A KIND OF FOLKLORE BEGAN TO ACCUMULATE AROUND IT. APPARENTLY IT WAS THE DREAM PROJECT OF A RECLUSIVE MULTIMILLIONAIRE.
HIS PHANTOM PRESENCE WAS ANNOUNCED BY THE APPEARANCE O AN ENORMOUS BLACK HUMMER. WE NEVER SAW THE VEHICLE MOTION. IT WAS EITHER THERE, OR NOT THERE, AS IF IT MATERIA IZED FROM ANOTHER DIMENSION.
CAREFUL! YOU'LL TRIGGER THE FORCE FIELD!
I JUST WANT SEE IF IT'S BIGGER ON THE INSIDE...
THE ORIGIN OF THE CONDO WAS SHROUDED IN MYSTERY. ACCORDING TO SOME LOCALS, THE MILLIONAIRE WAS IMPRESSED BY A SIMILAR STRUCTURE IN HIS NATIVE SHANGHAI.
HOW MUCH WOULD IT COST TO BUILD THAT IN THE U.S.?
NADINE WAS CONVINCED THAT HE WAS INSPIRED BY THE BEACH CONDOMINIUMS OF MIAMI. HE WAS STRUCK BY THE ACOUSTIC SIMILARITY BETWEEN OCEAN WAVES AND TRAFFIC FLOWS.
LISTEN... IT'S LIKE A HIGHWAY...
THE REAL REASON WAS PROBABLY FAR MORE BANAL AND FRIGHTENING, LIKE AN IMPULSE PURCHASE AT AN ARCHI TECTURAL WHOLESALER.
HMM... HOW MANY STORIES IS IT?
HIRISE CATALOG VOL 3
YOU CAN HAV AS MANY AS LOCAL PERMITS ALLOW...
NADINE'S PROPERTY WAS PROBABLY THE MOST AFFECTED BY THE CONSTRUCTION. AFTER LIVING IN THE NEIGHBORHOOD SINCE THE 1920s, HER SOUTHERN SUN EXPOSURE WAS NOW ENTIRELY BLOCKED.
HI NADINE.
I HOPE THAT STUPID CONDO DOESN'T FALL ON YOU!
GOD FORBID!
THIS SEASON, HER ANNUAL TOMATO AND CUCUMBER CROP FAILED TO DEVELOP.
POOR NADINE!
WHAT'S THAT?
THE CONDO ON THE OTHE HAND KEPT SPROUTING N MUTANT FLORA.
WE TOTALLY HAVE TO GO SOMETIME!
HIVIEW tower™ OPEN HOUSE SAT & SUN 1-4 FROM 976 SQ FT AFFORDABLE LUXURY

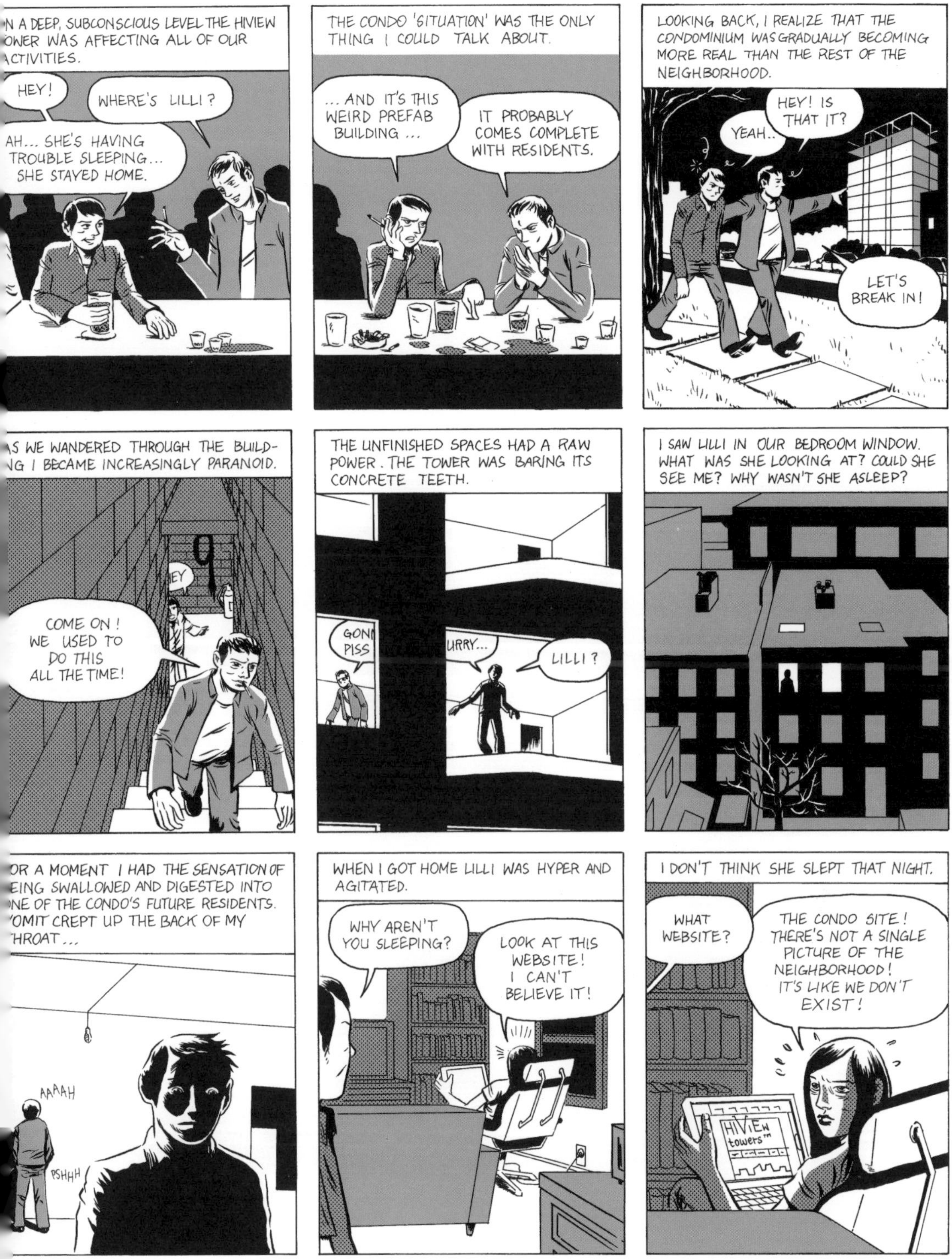
N A DEEP, SUBCONSCIOUS LEVEL THE HIVIEW
OWER WAS AFFECTING ALL OF OUR
CTIVITIES.
HEY!
WHERE'S LILLI?
AH... SHE'S HAVING TROUBLE SLEEPING... SHE STAYED HOME.
THE CONDO 'SITUATION' WAS THE ONLY THING I COULD TALK ABOUT.
...AND IT'S THIS WEIRD PREFAB BUILDING...
IT PROBABLY COMES COMPLETE WITH RESIDENTS.
LOOKING BACK, I REALIZE THAT THE CONDOMINIUM WAS GRADUALLY BECOMING MORE REAL THAN THE REST OF THE NEIGHBORHOOD.
HEY! IS THAT IT?
YEAH..
LET'S BREAK IN!
S WE WANDERED THROUGH THE BUILD-
G I BECAME INCREASINGLY PARANOID.
EY
COME ON! WE USED TO DO THIS ALL THE TIME!
THE UNFINISHED SPACES HAD A RAW POWER. THE TOWER WAS BARING ITS CONCRETE TEETH.
GON
PISS
URRY...
LILLI?
I SAW LILLI IN OUR BEDROOM WINDOW. WHAT WAS SHE LOOKING AT? COULD SHE SEE ME? WHY WASN'T SHE ASLEEP?
OR A MOMENT I HAD THE SENSATION OF
EING SWALLOWED AND DIGESTED INTO
NE OF THE CONDO'S FUTURE RESIDENTS.
OMIT CREPT UP THE BACK OF MY
HROAT...
AAAAH
PSHHH
WHEN I GOT HOME LILLI WAS HYPER AND AGITATED.
WHY AREN'T YOU SLEEPING?
LOOK AT THIS WEBSITE! I CAN'T BELIEVE IT!
I DON'T THINK SHE SLEPT THAT NIGHT.
WHAT WEBSITE?
THE CONDO SITE! THERE'S NOT A SINGLE PICTURE OF THE NEIGHBORHOOD! IT'S LIKE WE DON'T EXIST!
HIVIEW towers™

A FEW MONTHS LATER WE FINALLY GOT A CHANCE TO TAKE ADVANTAGE OF THE HIVIEW TOWER OPEN HOUSE.
...STYLE CABINETS WITH MATTE LACQUER FINISH. CUSTOM-QUARRIED IMHOTEP EGYPTIAN STONE COUNTERTOPS, COMPLEMENTED BY ICE-GLASS BACK...
THE POTENTIAL BUYERS WERE UNCOMFORTABLE. THEY SAW THEMSELVES AS SHOCK TROOPS OF GENTRIFICATION. ALL OF THEM WISHED THEY COULD AFFORD REAL ISLANDS INSTEAD OF BEIN STRANDED ON THIS CONCRETE REEF.
...HIVIEW TOWER WILL BRING UNDERSTATED ELEGANCE TO THE RAMBO STREETSCAPE MERGING URBAN GRIT WITH GLAMOUR...
THE WORDS OF THE SALES GIRL SOUNDED LIKE SOME KIND OF OTHER DIMENSIONAL JARGON. IT WAS AMUSING FOR A WHILE...
...SPA-STYLE MASTER BATHS PROVIDE A TRANQUIL RETREAT WITH HIGH END FINISHES. DURANGO STONE, CUBO FIXTURES, KTULU FAUCETS...
Please do not urinate here!
Por favor no orine aqui!
SOON A KIND OF CREEPINESS SET IN. THE MONOTONOUS DELIVERY OF THE SALES PITCH TOOK ON THE QUALITY OF A TRANCE-INDUCING CHANT.
...24 HOUR FULL SER CONCIERGE, FITNESS FACILITY ONSITE VA
SPACE BECAME CHARGED WITH LUMIN OTHERWORDLY ENERGY... GEOMETRY BEGAN TO FLUCTUATE... LILLI SEEMED MESMERIZED... DIAPHANOUS...
I KNEW THE ROOMS WERE EMPTY SHELLS OF CHEAP DRYWALL... BUT FOR AN INSTANT WE SAW SPECTERS OF DESIGNER FURNITURE...
OUTSIDE, AN UNFAMILIAR VISTA UNFOLDED.
WHAT HAPPENED TO THE NEIGHBORHOOD?
AFFORDABLE LUXURY IS A HERMETIC UTOPIA. A NEIGHBORHOOD IS UNNECESSA
...AND A COURTESY SHUTTLE TO THE SUBWAY!
AND DON'T FORGET THE COMPLIMENTARY HIVIEW MUGS!

HE HIVIEW TOWER OPEN HOUSE ACTED
S SOME KIND OF TRIGGER.
WHOA!
THEY'VE TAKEN THE SKY!
LILLI'S SLEEP BECAME MORE ERRATIC. SHE BECAME OBSESSED WITH MYSPACE.
YOU HAVE TO SLEEP!
BE RIGHT THERE, CHECKING FOR NEW COMMENTS...
HER MENTAL SPACE HAD BEEN INVADED... IN RETROSPECT, DEFENDING HER MYSPACE TURF WAS A FORM OF RETALIATION.
I THINK I KNOW WHO HACKED INTO MY ACCOUNT...
UT IT WAS A LOSING BATTLE. HER DEFENSES
ERE RUN OVER BY CORPORATE CHIEFTAINS
FFLUENT PROGRESSIVES, BOURGEOIS BO-
EMIANS, AND OTHER DEMOGRAPHIC DEMONS.
AKE UP!
HUH?
THEY'RE MOVING IN! WE HAVE TO LEAVE!
HER MIND FRACTURED INTO AN ARCHITECTURE OF CONSUMER PREFERENCES. EACH CONDO UNIT A UNIQUE MARKETING HABITUS. 976 SQ.FT. OF MYSPACE.
SHE WAS THE RECIPIENT OF AN ENDLESS FLOOD OF PSYCHIC JUNK MAIL... I GAVE HER 50 MG OF DIPHENHYDRAMINE.
TAKE THIS...
SHOULD I APPLY FOR A STRESS-FREE HOME-EQUITY LOAN...?
HE DRUG ONLY EXACERBATED LILLI'S
ONDITION. AT THIS POINT, AFTER THREE
AYS OF INSOMNIA, SHE EQUATED SLEEP
ITH DEFEAT AND DEATH.
RE ARE YOU?
LET ME
ASLEEP
SHE WAS FIGHTING HER WAY OUT OF A LABYRINTH OF 24 HOUR ATTENDED LOBBIES. EACH ONE BOASTING DRAMATIC DOUBLE-HEIGHT CEILINGS, FIREPLACE...
EXOTIC WOODS ELEGANT IVORY LIMESTONE WALLS AND FLOORS...
HER EXISTENTIAL FOUNDATIONS WERE LOST IN AN AMORPHOUS MIASMA OF JUNK SPACE.
ENJOY MAGNIFICENT, SWEEPING VIEWS THROUGH HUGE DOUBLE PANED WINDOWS...
UH... I NEED AN AMBULANCE...
OR AN ARCHITECT...

I FOUND OUT LATER THAT THE NEIGHBORHOOD WAS SWEPT BY AN EPIDEMIC OF UNUSUAL EVENTS AS A RESULT OF THE CONDO-ALTERED PSYCHOGEOGRAPHY.
SOME PEOPLE MOVED SUDDENLY, OFFERING NO EXPLANATION. THERE WAS A SERIOUS OUTBREAK OF SAD.* NADINE WAS AMONG THOSE STRUCK. HER BLIND HUSBAND ASSUMED TRIPPY DUTY.
TAK TAK
TAK
IT'S PAINFUL TO TO WATCH...
*SEASONAL AFFECTIVE DISORDER
ONE BUILDING BURNED DOWN DUE TO CO
STRUCTION ERROR... CONVENIENTLY MAKI
ROOM FOR A NEW CONDO. THERE WERE MANY MORE INCIDENTS TOO NUMEROUS TO MENTION.
SOME SEEMED TO BENEFIT FROM THE CONDO CURSE. TRIPPY'S OWNER WAS ONE OF THE FEW WHO DECIDED TO MOVE INTO THE TOWER.
WHY DOESN'T SHE EVER WALK HER DOG?
BUT IN A SENSE EVERYONE ELSE MOVED IN, TOO... THOSE THAT HAVEN'T YET WILL SOON. AND THEY WILL FORGET WHAT THE BLOCK LOOKED LIKE BEFORE THE TOWER...
HI VIEW
555 5555
FROM 976 SQ FT
AFFORDABLE LUXURY
GEOGRAPHICAL AMNESIA WILL SUTURE THE FRAGMENTED SPATIAL MEMORY. THE SCAR TISSUE TRANSFORMED INTO NEW FLESH.
HOSPITAL
PSYCH WAR
9th floor
PSYCHIATRY TODAY
THE DOCTORS HAD LOTS OF THEORIES EXPLAINING LILLI'S SUDDEN DERANGEMENT. BIPOLAR DISORDER, HASHIMOTO'S DISEASE, MUNCHAUSEN SYNDROME. THE LIST WENT ON.
BUT THEY DIDN'T SEE THE CONDOMINIUM... AFTER DAYS OF FUTILE PSYCHIATRIC OBSERVATION, LILLI WAS ABOUT TO BE DISCHARGED.
THE CITY OUTSIDE WAS DOTTED WITH NEW
CONDO CONSTRUCTION. HER EYES TOLD M
THAT THIS ROOM WAS GOING TO BE HER HO
FOR A LONG TIME...
I WAS TEMPTED TO JOIN HER.

YOU CAN RECOGNIZE THE MOMENT ALMOST NSTANTLY. THOSE ALREADY ASLEEP ARE JARRED AWAKE.
2:26 AM
WHAT YOU NOTICE IS THE LACK OF SOUND. THE CONSTANT DIN OF CIVILIZATION HAS GROUND TO A HALT. EVEN THE FRIDGE STOPPED PURRING REASSURINGLY. IS THIS JUST A NORMAL FLUCTUATION OF THE POWER GRID?
THEN YOU NOTICE THE INSECTS. SCREECHING SWARMS... OBLIVIOUS TO YOUR PRESENCE. HOW MANY ARE THERE? THEY WERE HERE BEFORE MANKIND. THEY WILL STILL BE HERE AFTER HUMANS GO EXTINCT.
E CARDIOVASCULAR SYSTEM RESPONDS. OOD RUSHES THROUGH THE VEINS WITH ADENING VIOLENCE ACTIVATING OBSCURE ANDS AND LONG FORGOTTEN SENSORY RGANS.
WHITE NOISE
THE IMPERCEPTIBLE TECTONIC DRIFT COMES INTO SHARP RELIEF... CONTINENTAL SHELVES CRASH INTO EACH OTHER... ANCIENT REMAINS SHIFT UNEASILY BENEATH EARTH'S CRUST...
GRIND
U CAN EVEN HEAR THE FAINT RADIO HUM DISTANT SUPERNOVAS TRAVELLING FOR ONS THROUGH DEAD SPACE AHEAD OF E SILENT SCREAMS OF ALIEN WORLDS...
IGULFED IN UNTLESS SOLAR HOLOCAUSTS...
CLACK
WHHHRRRR
clyde
WHHHRRRRrr
ZZZZZ

SPACE

100,000 MILES

10,000 Miles

C 0
M 0
Y 85
K 15

PHASE TRANSITION

First appearance: *MOME 10*, 2008

1,000 Miles

100 Miles

1 Mile

1,000,000,000 BC   1,000,000 BC   500,000 BC   40,000

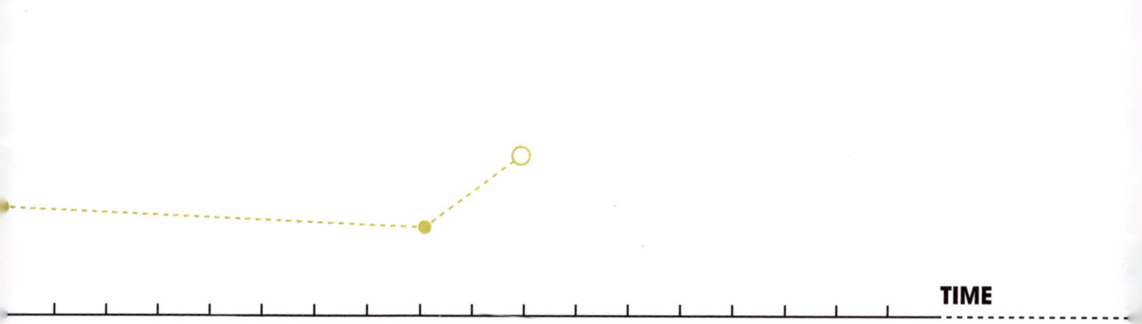
TIME
2000 AD
10, 000 AD

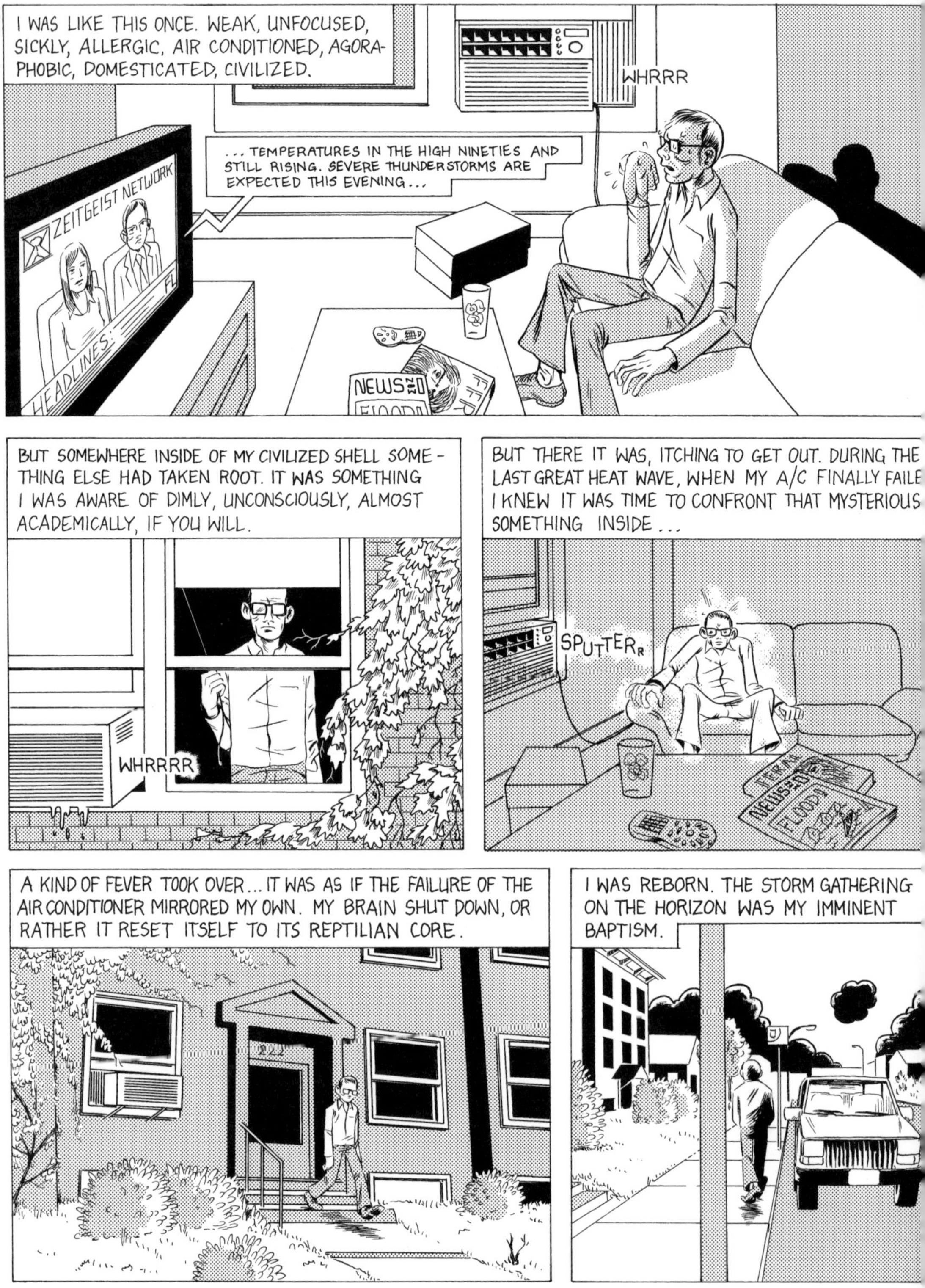
I WAS LIKE THIS ONCE. WEAK, UNFOCUSED, SICKLY, ALLERGIC, AIR CONDITIONED, AGORAPHOBIC, DOMESTICATED, CIVILIZED.
WHRRR
... TEMPERATURES IN THE HIGH NINETIES AND STILL RISING. SEVERE THUNDERSTORMS ARE EXPECTED THIS EVENING...
ZEITGEIST NETWORK
HEADLINES:
NEWS
BUT SOMEWHERE INSIDE OF MY CIVILIZED SHELL SOMETHING ELSE HAD TAKEN ROOT. IT WAS SOMETHING I WAS AWARE OF DIMLY, UNCONSCIOUSLY, ALMOST ACADEMICALLY, IF YOU WILL.
WHRRRR
BUT THERE IT WAS, ITCHING TO GET OUT. DURING THE LAST GREAT HEAT WAVE, WHEN MY A/C FINALLY FAILE
I KNEW IT WAS TIME TO CONFRONT THAT MYSTERIOUS SOMETHING INSIDE...
SPUTTERR
NEWS
FLOOD
A KIND OF FEVER TOOK OVER... IT WAS AS IF THE FAILURE OF THE AIR CONDITIONER MIRRORED MY OWN. MY BRAIN SHUT DOWN, OR RATHER IT RESET ITSELF TO ITS REPTILIAN CORE.
I WAS REBORN. THE STORM GATHERING ON THE HORIZON WAS MY IMMINENT BAPTISM.

I CAN NOW SAY WITH CERTAINTY THAT I WAS FOLLOWING A PATH.
EACH STEP EXHUMED SUPPRESSED MEMORIES, WHICH IN TURN, EXCAVATED FOUNDATIONS OF FORGOTTEN CITIES BURIED BY INCESSANT DAILY ROUTINES.
26R
WHEN WAS THE LAST TIME I TOOK THIS BUS LINE?
MY MIND AND THE CITY COLLAPSED INTO EACH OTHER.
26R
THE BUS ALLOWED GREATER TEMPORAL DISTANCES.
EACH BUS STOP WAS A DISCARDED LIFE.
EACH DISTRICT AN EON.
I RODE UNTIL THE END OF HISTORY...
DING
... OR THE BEGINNING. DEPENDS ON WHOM YOU ASK.
26R
ON THE HORIZON LOOMED CONCRETE SENTINELS. THE SCENT OF DESTINY PERMEATED THE AIR. MY RIGHT ARM SUDDENLY BEGAN TO ITCH.
SKRITCH SKRITCH

WHEN I WAS YOUNG I IMAGINED THE GRAIN SILOS TO BE ARTIFACTS FROM SOME ANTEDILUVIAN CIVILIZATION. THEY SEEMED IMPROBABLY ARCHAIC IN THEIR DECAYING SPLENDOR.
THEY WERE MY PYRAMIDS OF EGYPT FILLED WITH ARCANE MYSTERIES. MY RETURN TO THIS CHARGED PLACE SIGNALE
MY ARRIVAL AT THE THRESHOLD OF DISCOVERY.
THE COMPLEX WAS GUARDED BY A MONSTER... A FERAL CREATURE, FIERCELY TERRITORIAL.
WHEN I SAW THE DOG I THOUGHT I WAS EXPERIENCING A HEAT-INDUCED MIRAGE.
UH...
SCRITCH SCRITCH
THE PHYSIOLOGY OF FEAR IS ANIMAL, INVOLUNTARY, EYES WIDEN. PUPILS DILATE. EYEBROWS DRAW TOGETHER. THE UPPER LIP RISES...
SCRITCH SCRITCH
OLD SCARS ITCH WITH REMEMBERED PAIN... THE PSYCHOLOGY OF FEAR IS A DIFFERENT BEAST.
SCARS BECOME HIEROGLYPHS. REPRESSED TRAUMA BECOMES THE ROSETTA STONE.

BUT THIS FEAR IS ONLY A SCREEN, A DECOY.	THE DOG BITE I EXPERIENCED AS A CHILD WAS ONLY THE LITERAL, PHYSICAL EVENT.	BELOW IS THE PRIMAL NIGHTMARE OF THE HUMAN SPECIES: THE FEAR OF NATURE.	BUT THIS IS WHAT WE HIDE BEHIND WHEN WE TAME, DOMESTICATE, AND CIVILIZE.

"AAAHH"

"STAY!"

IN THAT BRIEF MOMENT, LOOKING INTO THE EYES OF THE DOG, I SAW MYSELF STANDING BEHIND THAT SCREEN. I WAS NAKED, STRONG, UNTAMED, FERAL... A WILD ANIMAL... FREE FROM THE TRAUMA OF CIVILIZATION.

I KNOW THAT THE ANIMAL SAW THE BEAST INSIDE ME. WE SAW EACH OTHER AS IF IN A MIRROR.

BY THE TIME I NOTICED THE RAIN I WAS ALREADY CHANGED.

AS I WALKED AMONG THE CONCRETE RUINS, I KNEW THIS WASN'T AN ORDINARY SEVERE THUNDERSTORM.

THIS WAS A SAVAGE TORRENT, A PRELUDE TO A GREAT DELUGE THAT WILL DROWN THIS ROTTING WORLD, THIS FETID CIVILIZATION. AND I... I WAS ITS CENTER.

TOM K.

NOISE a history

BANG. 14 BILLION BC. ? DB

WATERFALL. 80,000 BC. 60 DB

SANTORINI ERUPTION. 1650 BC. 200 DB

THE TURKISH BOMBARD AT THE SIEGE OF CONSTANTINOPLE. 1453 AD. 120 DB

TWENTIETH CENTURY LIMITED. NORTH AMERICA. 1905 AD. 95 DB

RUSTLING OF LEAVES. CENTRAL PARK. 1885 AD. 10 DB

SYMPHONY OF THE CITY. 1914 AD. 95 DB

NUCLEAR EXPLOSION. NAGASAKI. 1945 AD. 248 DB

PERSONAL AUDIO DEVICE. NOW. 90 DB

T. KACZYNSKI

53

SPACE

100,000 MILES

10,000 Miles

C 0
M 0
Y 85
K 15

MILLION YEAR BOOM

First appearance: *MOME 11*, 2008
Reprinted in *Best American Nonrequired Reading*, 2009

1,000 Miles

100 Miles

1 Mile

1,000,000,000 BC   1,000,000 BC   500,000 BC   40,000

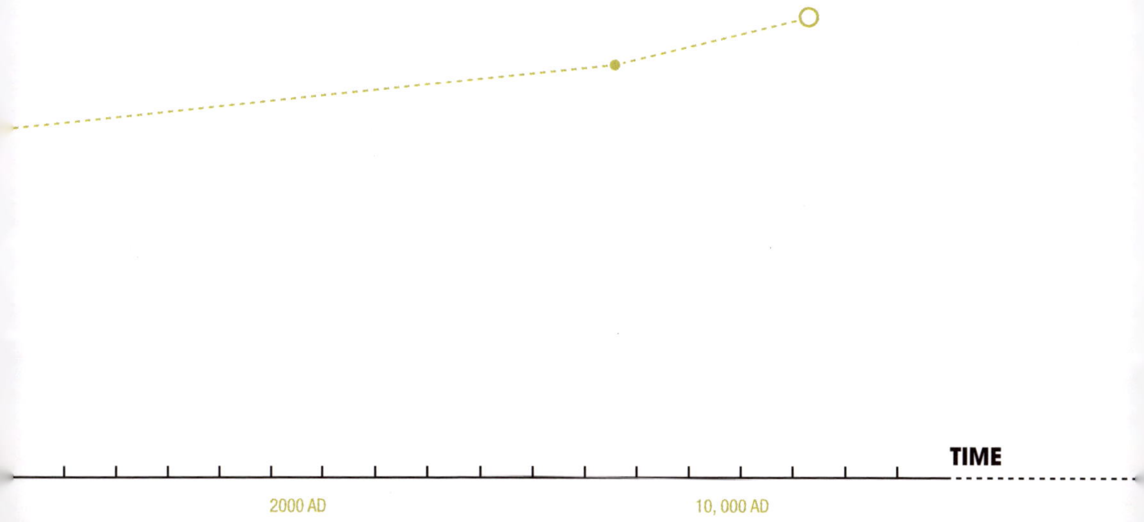

TIME
2000 AD
10, 000 AD

FULLY, MY EARS FAILED TO POP AFTER THE LANDING.

EVERYTHING SOUNDED MUTED AND DISTANT. I FELT LIKE A DEEP SEA DIVER DESCENDING INTO A BOTTOMLESS OCEANIC TRENCH.

MY CAB WAS A BATHYSPHERE STUMBLING UPON SOME ANCIENT SUBMERGED CIVILIZATION.

THE SILENCE OF MY DESCENT WAS INTERRUPTED ONLY BY THE TAXI'S RADIO, WHICH, DURING COMMERCIAL BREAKS BECAME ALMOST AUDIBLE.

THE DESPERATE PITCH OF THE ADS MADE THEM SOUND LIKE CRYPTIC WARNINGS FROM AN INCREASINGLY DISTANT SURFACE WORLD.

WAS I BEING RECALLED TO THE SURFACE?

MY UNDERWATER REVERIE WAS INTERRUPTED BY MY ARRIVAL AT **THE WILDERNESS ESTATES**. THIS WAS A GATED CORPORATE HOUSING COMPLEX AND IT WAS GOING TO BE MY HOME FOR THE NEXT SEVERAL WEEKS.
leasing office
BUILDING 2, SECOND FLOOR, APARTMENT 26.
WHAT? OH... THANKS.
@HOME IN THE WILD
WILDERNESS ESTATES BULLETIN
THE NAME OF THE PLACE SEEMED A BIT OFF. PERHAPS **WILDERNESS** SIMPLY DENOTED THE ABSENCE OF A CIVILIZING METROPOLIS? WHAT KIND OF **SAVAGES** INHABITED ULTRA-MODERNIST MACHINES FOR LIVING?
OOOF...
MY NEW EMPLOYER LEFT ME A STRANGE NOTE...
...A GREAT TRIP. PLEASE TAKE ADVANTAGE OF ALL THE AMENITIES TO CLEANSE YOUR BODY & SOUL. YOU WILL NEED ALL YOUR STRENGTH TO JOIN US ON THIS EXTRAORDINARY JOURNEY! –R. RAFFERTY, PHD.
?
OW! WHY WON'T THEY POP?
... WHO'S DR. RAFFERTY?
I DECIDED TO FOLLOW THE DOCTOR'S ADVICE.
WUW ... WHO'S THAT?
MY EARS FINALLY POPPED WHEN I HIT THE WATER.
PLISH

IE COMPANY WAS A HOT START-UP TRYING TO MAKE ITS MARK ON THE NEW
REEN ECONOMY. THEIR BUSINESS WAS DIFFICULT TO DEFINE, AS THEY
EMED TO HAVE THEIR TENTACLES IN A WIDE VARIETY OF INDUSTRIES.
IT WAS LOCATED IN THE FORMER HEADQUARTERS OF A ONCE INVINCIBLE INTERNET GIANT. BUT, THE COMPANY'S GLOBAL AMBITIONS, EMBODIED IN THE HUGE CAMPUS, WERE MARRED BY A LACK OF CLEAR CORPORATE IDENTITY.
SENTIALLY, THE COMPANY WAS A GROUP OF HIPPY
ENTISTS, LAWYERS AND MANAGERS, DROWNING
INVESTOR CAPITAL, OPERATING UNDER THE
NNER OF A CLIP-ART SQUID.
I'M HERE TO SEE MR. LUBBOCK.
HE'S IN CONFERENCE ROOM 23.
THE COMPANY WAS ABOUT TO GO PUBLIC AND NEEDED A NEW IMAGE, A NEW BRAND TO CHARM THE DEMONIC MARKET FORCES IN THEIR FAVOUR.
I WAS HIRED AS PART OF A SMALL TEAM OF BRAND EXPERTS. IT TOOK ME A LONG TIME TO COME UP WITH A REASON TO SIGN UP...
CR-23
KNOCK KNOCK
E ALMOST EVERYONE HERE, I DIDN'T WANT TO LEAVE A COMFORTABLE COSMOPOLITAN CITY LIFE
THIS UNCERTAIN SUBURBAN ENTERPRISE. I CAN'T SPEAK FOR THE OTHERS...
... A GRAPHIC SOLUTION TO THE BEGINNING OF A NEW AEON ...
LOOK WHO FINALLY DECIDED TO JOIN US!
... BUT IN THE END I COULDN'T RESIST HAVING A HAND IN THE CREATION OF THE MYTHOLOGY OF THE NEXT GREAT GLOBAL CORPORATION...
CR-23
HI GUYS!

AT THE END OF MY FIRST DAY, LUBBOCK GAVE ME A TOUR OF THE COMPANY COMPLEX.
... THE GROUNDS ARE SOME OF THE MOST ENVIRONMENTALLY ADVANCED IN THE COUNTRY. THIS ISN'T YOUR TYPICAL CORPORATE HQ SITTING ON THE ECOLOGICAL EQUIVALENT OF A GOLF COURSE!
LUBBOCK SLIPPED INTO THE ROLE OF A TOUR GUIDE EFFORTLESSLY AND WI THE CONVICTION OF A NATIVE. HIS EASY FAMILIARITY WITH THE ANCIENT HISTORY OF THE AREA GAVE HIM THE AURA OF A STONE AGE WISE MAN.
THE LAWN, IF YOU CAN CALL IT THAT, IS A CLOSE RECONSTRUCTION OF THE MIX OF PLANTS THAT GRE IN THE AREA UNTIL THEY WERE DISPLACED BY THE ADVENT OF AGRICULTURE...
UH, HUH
OVER HERE IS A FRAGMENT OF THE ABORIGINAL DECIDUOUS FOREST. WE WANT IT TO GROW FURTHER! WE'RE ALL TREE HUGGERS HERE!
BUT THEY SERVE A VALUABLE FUNCTION AS WELL. THE TREES ARE A REFUGE FOR SEVERAL ENDANGERED SPECIES. THEY COME HERE TO FIND SHELTER FROM HUMANS AND EXTREME WEATHER... IN A WAY WE'RE NOT SO DIFFERENT FROM THEM...
WE'VE BUILT UP QUITE A PLEASANT MICRO-CLIMATE HERE... OH...
LOOK HERE!
HUH?
THIS IS ERUCA INGENIUM! ONE OF THE RAREST AND MOST VALUABLE FLORA! IT'S NEARLY EXTINCT...
HUH?! WHY'D YOU PICK IT?
TSK! NO WORRIES! THERE IT'S SAFELY BACK IN THE GROUND... IT WOULDN'T BE WORTH ANYTHING IF WE DIDN'T EVER PICK IT... THAT'S WHY WE'RE HERE, TO INJECT SOME ECONOMIC VALUE INTO ALL THIS WILD SPLENDOR!
AAAHHHHHHACHOO
PAT PAT PAT
GESUNDHEIT...
AND OVER HERE IS THE...
WHAT'S WITH THE STONE CIRCLES?
SNIFF

E PACE OF WORK WAS INTENSE. LATE NIGHTS
D WEEKEND WORK WERE STANDARD. THE ENORMITY
THE COMPANY'S PROJECT BECAME QUICKLY
PARENT.
NIFF... WE NEED A SYMBOLIC
NTAINER THAT CAN HOLD
H... ARCHAIC HERITAGE
D.. SNIFF... THE LIMITLESS
SIBILITIES OF THE FUTURE...
UGH... I THINK I'M GETTING A COLD...
IN SHORT THE COMPANY WAS ATTEMPTING TO MAP THE ENTIRE PRODUCTIVITY OF THE PLANET'S BIOSPHERE INTO DOLLAR TERMS... EVENTUALLY THIS WOULD LEAD TO THE CREATION OF A NEW GLOBAL BIO-CURRENCY...
... SO EVEN A BLADE OF GRASS WOULD HAVE, SNIFF, EXCHANGE VALUE?
TO GET A MORE ACCURATE MEASURE OF THE PERFORMANCE OF THE GLOBAL BIO-ECONOMY, THE COMPANY WAS RETROACTIVELY PROJECTING CONTEMPORARY MARKET ECONOMICS INTO A MILLION YEARS OF PLANETARY HISTORY.
MY COLD IS GETTING WORSE.
SNIFF
KLACK KLACK
WAS ENOUGH TO MAKE ANYONE'S HEAD SPIN...
D I WAS ALREADY DIZZY FROM WHAT SEEMED
E A NASTY SINUS INFECTION.
SMOKE BREAK?
SNIFF... SURE!
...YOU HAVEN'T COME TO ANY OF THE SPECIAL CREATIVITY SESSIONS YET...
AAAHHCHOO
GESUNDHEIT
YOU OK?
YEAH... I JUST HAVE THIS PERPETUAL CONGESTION... IT'S PROBABLY JUST A COLD OR SOMETHING...
MHMM...
SNIFF
... I HAD SOMETHING SIMILAR WHEN I STARTED HERE... TURNED OUT TO BE A RARE ALLERGY CAUSED BY AN ENDANGERED PLANT... I GUESS IT'S HAPPENED TO OTHERS, TOO...
REALLY?
YEAH... YOU SHOULD SEE DOCTOR RAFFERTY ABOUT IT.
SNIFF, I DON'T LIKE DOCTORS... I'VE NEVER BEEN ALLERGIC TO ANYTHING BEFORE... BESIDES ISN'T HE A SHRINK?
I HADN'T MET DOCTOR RAFFERTY YET, BUT I NOTICED HOW HIS NAME WAS ALWAYS INVOKED WITH A HUSHED AWE...
YEAH HE'S A SHRINK... BUT HE'S ALSO MUCH MORE THAN THAT... GO SEE HIM.
I'M SURE I'LL GET BETTER SOON...
SNIFF

OVER THE NEXT FEW DAYS I WAS REMINDED OF MY INITIAL MISGIVINGS ABOUT LEAVING THE RELATIVE SAFETY OF THE BIG CITY.
UGH... THESE MEDS AREN'T HELPING MUCH ... MAYBE THIS **IS** SOME KIND OF WEIRD ALLERGY ... ?
SNIFF
THE CORPORATE HOUSING COMPLEX ACTED AS A KIND OF STERILE DEPRIVATION CHAMBER IN CONTRAST TO THE SENSORY RICHNESS OF THE ECOLOGICAL EDEN SURROUNDING THE COMPANY CAMPUS.
THAT LAMP GIVES ME THE CREEPS...
COLD & SINUS
THE COCKTAIL OF SUBURBAN ISOLATION AND **NON-DROWSY** COLD MEDICATION WAS DEADLY. I WAS SLOWLY GOING OUT OF MY MIND.
WHO WOULD EVER NAME THIS PLACE THE WILDERNESS ESTATES ... !?
CLICK
CLICK
CLICK
THE ONLY ANTIDOTE AGAINST CRUSHING BOREDOM WAS PHYSICAL EXERTION. I BECAME OBSESSED WITH SWIMMING.
I WOULD SWIM UNTIL COMPLETE EXHAUSTION ... THEN, DRAINED, I WOULD FLOAT, **SUSPENDED** PRECARIOUSLY IN THE MIDDLE OF A GENTLE TUG OF WAR BETWEEN GRAVITY AND WATER ... THE FAINT CHEMICAL ODOR OF CHLORINE KEEPING MY CONGESTION AT BAY...
EXIT
MY ONLY SPECTATOR WAS A BEAUTIFUL WOMAN WHO REGARDED MY PRESE WITH THE KIND OF ATTENTION USUALLY RESERVED FOR DRIFTWOOD.
WHAT'S HER STORY ?

STILL SUFFERING?
SNIFF... YEAH... UM... I THINK YOU MIGHT BE RIGHT.
LISTEN, HERE'S WHAT RAFFERTY GAVE ME FOR THIS ALLERGY. I HAVE A COUPLE OF PILLS LEFT. YOU SHOULD TRY THEM.
BUT DON'T YOU NEED THEM?
I CAN ALWAYS GET MORE.
YOU WON'T REGRET IT! AND GO SEE THE DOCTOR!
THANKS
NIUM
UPLE OF HOURS LATER THE DICATION KICKED IN. ALL MPTOMS VANISHED.
...ODD, MY FINGERS ARE TINGLING...
KLACK KLACK KLACK
MORE THAN THAT, ONCE THE SINUS HAZE CLEARED, MY BODY WENT INTO SENSORY OVERDRIVE.
I THINK I'M GETTING HIGH FROM THESE DRY ERASE MARKERS
SQUEEEEEK
HA HA HA
SIMPLE ACTIVITIES LIKE EATING ACQUIRED NEW IMPORTANCE. I CHEWED WITH DETERMINATION.
TASTES LIKE SHIT... BUT I CAN **TASTE** IT...
CHEW CHEW
VMMMMM...
VMMMMM
ENETRATED THE STILL SURFACE THE POOL, EAGER TO IMMERSE SELF IN THE COOL **DEPTHS**.
PLISH
MY LIMBS **FLAILED** WITH WILD ABANDON IN AN ATTEMPT TO **AGITATE** NOT ONLY THE STAGNANT WATER BUT ALSO MY **INERT** AUDIENCE.
BUT SHE WAS UNMOVED BY MY **PHYSICAL DISPLAYS**. WHAT WOULD IT TAKE TO DISTURB HER UN-BREAKABLE POISE?
I WOKE UP TIRED AND **DRAINED**. THE ALLERGY SYMPTOMS RETURNED.
I HAVE TO GET MORE OF THAT MEDICATION.
SNIFF
SCRITCH SCRITCH

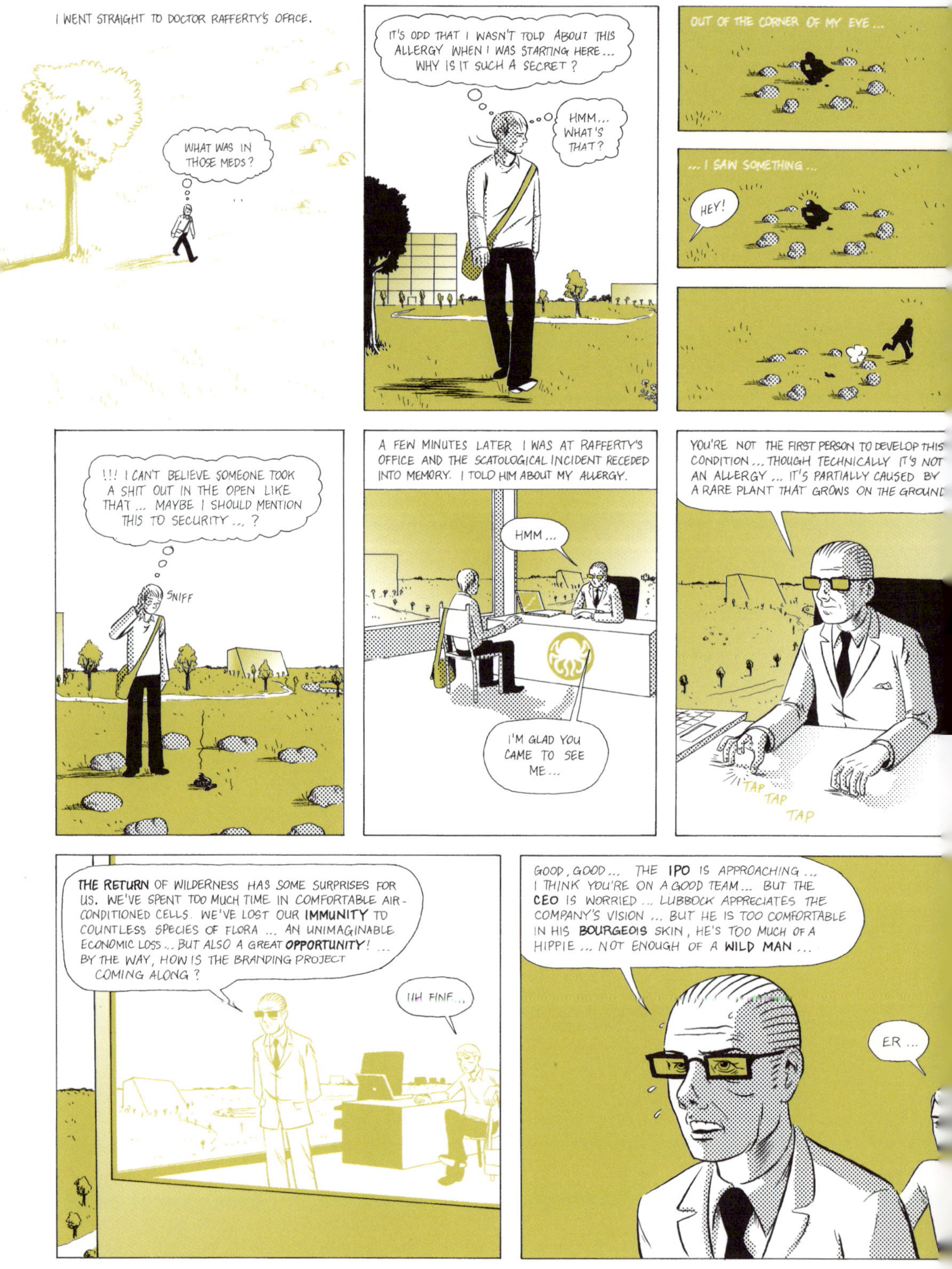
I WENT STRAIGHT TO DOCTOR RAFFERTY'S OFFICE.
WHAT WAS IN THOSE MEDS?
IT'S ODD THAT I WASN'T TOLD ABOUT THIS ALLERGY WHEN I WAS STARTING HERE... WHY IS IT SUCH A SECRET?
HMM... WHAT'S THAT?
OUT OF THE CORNER OF MY EYE...
... I SAW SOMETHING...
HEY!
!!! I CAN'T BELIEVE SOMEONE TOOK A SHIT OUT IN THE OPEN LIKE THAT... MAYBE I SHOULD MENTION THIS TO SECURITY...?
SNIFF
A FEW MINUTES LATER I WAS AT RAFFERTY'S OFFICE AND THE SCATOLOGICAL INCIDENT RECEDED INTO MEMORY. I TOLD HIM ABOUT MY ALLERGY.
HMM...
I'M GLAD YOU CAME TO SEE ME...
YOU'RE NOT THE FIRST PERSON TO DEVELOP THIS CONDITION... THOUGH TECHNICALLY IT'S NOT AN ALLERGY... IT'S PARTIALLY CAUSED BY A RARE PLANT THAT GROWS ON THE GROUND
TAP TAP TAP
THE RETURN OF WILDERNESS HAS SOME SURPRISES FOR US. WE'VE SPENT TOO MUCH TIME IN COMFORTABLE AIR-CONDITIONED CELLS. WE'VE LOST OUR IMMUNITY TO COUNTLESS SPECIES OF FLORA... AN UNIMAGINABLE ECONOMIC LOSS... BUT ALSO A GREAT OPPORTUNITY!... BY THE WAY, HOW IS THE BRANDING PROJECT COMING ALONG?
UH FINE...
GOOD, GOOD... THE IPO IS APPROACHING... I THINK YOU'RE ON A GOOD TEAM... BUT THE CEO IS WORRIED... LUBBOCK APPRECIATES THE COMPANY'S VISION... BUT HE IS TOO COMFORTABLE IN HIS BOURGEOIS SKIN, HE'S TOO MUCH OF A HIPPIE... NOT ENOUGH OF A WILD MAN...
ER...

THE FUTURE IS NOT ABOUT WEARING SANDALS, GREEN TIE-DYE T-SHIRTS AND FEELING ALL WARM AND FUZZY INSIDE... IN SOME WAYS THE GREEN ECONOMY MAY TURN OUT TO BE FAR MORE SAVAGE THAN WE IMAGINE... CAN THE ANTIDOTE BE WORSE THAN THE POISON? HAVE YOU STUMBLED ON ANY ANIMAL TRACKS LATELY?
UH WHAT?
?
NEVER MIND..., I HAVE ANOTHER APPOINTMENT NOW... I WILL GET YOU YOUR MEDICATION NOW...
SNIFF, THANKS...
Y REVITALIZED SENSES DRAGGED ME OUT THE FILTERED AIR OF THE CUBICLES.
WHAT DID HE MEAN BY "TECHNICALLY IT'S NOT AN ALLERGY"..?
KLACK KLACK KLACK
I DECIDED TO FAMILIARIZE MYSELF WITH THE GROUNDS. DURING BREAKS I EXPLORED THE OLD FOREST. I BECAME CONVINCED THE SOLUTION TO THE COMPANY'S BRAND LAY SOMEWHERE IN ITS DENSE THICKET.
MAYBE I'LL FIND THOSE TRACKS...
I CAME UPON MORE FECES. WERE VAGRANTS AMONG THE ENDANGERED SPECIES SHELTERED BY THE TREES? DID THE COMPANY HAVE A SECURITY PROBLEM?
DEFINITELY HUMAN, SIMILAR ODOR AS BEFORE.
NEW MOBILITY ALLOWED ME TO TAKE PART IN OUTDOOR CREATIVITY AND AM BUILDING EXERCISES. APPARENTLY THEY WERE ONE OF RAFFERTY'S NY MANAGERIAL INNOVATIONS.
THE STONE CIRCLES MYSTERY SOLVED!
OOF!
PERHAPS WE SHOULD TRY CAVE PAINTING INSTEAD?
WHEN THE STONE CIRCLE WAS FINISHED, I RESTED. MY ELEVATED HEARTBEAT REMINDED ME OF RAFFERTY'S TAPPING FINGER... FOR THE FIRST TIME I BEGAN TO UNDERSTAND THE FUTURE THE COMPANY WAS ENGINEERING.

AT HOME I SPENT MORE AND MORE TIME IN THE POOL. I WAS DRAWN TO ITS AUSTERE EMPTINESS, A MODERNIST WOMB. MY BODY DISSOLVED IN ITS AMNIOTIC FLUID INTO AN ALCHEMY OF AMINO ACIDS.

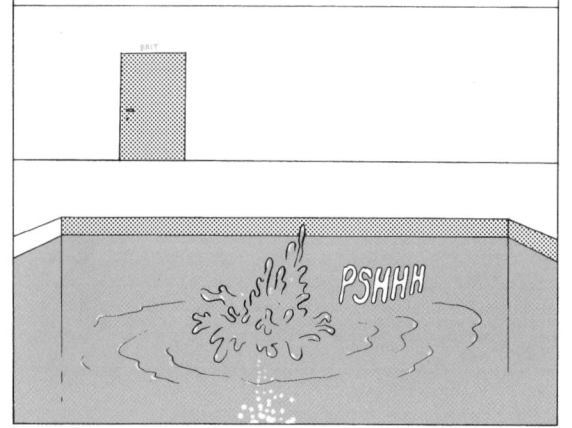

PSHHH

THIS IS HOW I IMAGINED THE PRIMORDIAL SOUP OF LIFE... A CHEMICAL CONSCIOUSNESS UNFORMED, UNBURDENED BY EVOLUTION, NOT YET READY TO SEIZE THE OFFERINGS OF THE COSMOS, BUT ALREADY FLUSH WITH GENETIC DESIRE.

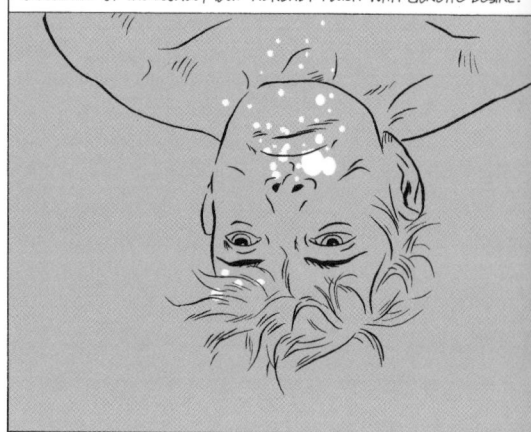

INSIDE I WOULD UNDERGO A DAILY IN VITRO MORPHOGENESIS... A SERIES OF MUTATIONS... THE GENETIC EQUIVALENT OF RAPID PROTOTYPING. I LEARNED TO BREATHE UNDERWATER. MY VISION ADJUSTED TO FLUID DISTORTIONS.

RELUCTANTLY I WOULD RETURN TO THE SURFACE. I KNEW THAT EVENTUALLY I WOULD HAVE TO RE-LEARN TO WALK ON LAND... NOT BECAUSE I LOST THAT ABILITY BUT BECAUSE THE LAND WILL HAVE TRANSFORMED, TOO...

DID I IMAGINE HER?

A FEW DAYS LATER RAFFERTY CALLED A MEETING. THE EMAIL INVITE ENDED WITH A QUOTE BY SIGMUND FREUD: "ANATOMY IS DESTINY." I SUSPECTED THIS WAS A NOT-SO-VEILED ATTEMPT TO RALLY THE STRUGGLING BRAND TEAM.

HE DOCTOR TRANSFORMED ON STAGE...
SUCCESS. VISION. ENERGY. ASK YOURSELVES THIS : WHO ARE YOUR ANCESTORS ? GENERAL ELECTRIC, FORD, IBM, APPLE, SONY, MICROSOFT GOOGLE ? NO! YOUR ANCESTORS ARE THE HUNTER-GATHERERS OF THE PALEOLITHIC WHO INVENTED LANGUAGE, MUSIC, AND ART!
THE AUDIENCE WAS MESMERIZED BY THE PERFORMANCE. I BECAME AWARE OF FAINT DRUMMING.
WE'RE ON THE VERGE OF THE GREATEST COMMERCIAL OPPORTUNITY IN HUMAN HISTORY. CARBON TRADE, BIO-FUELS, SOLAR ENERGY, THESE ARE ALL INSIGNIFICANT PUDDLES COMPARED TO THE VAST OCEANS OF PROFITS TO BE EXTRACTED FROM THIS PLANET...
AS I HEARING A RECORDED SOUNDTRACK OR THE THROBBING BLOOD RAFFERTY'S VEINS ?
HE COMING AGE OF CLIMATE DISASTERS WILL TEST THE INGENUITY THE SPECIES. WILL WE ACCEPT EXTINCTION LIKE THE NEADERTHALS?
AT SOME POINT I STOPPED LISTENING. I ALREADY KNEW WHAT RAFFERTY WAS GOING TO SAY, I HEARD IT BEFORE... IN THE POOL... WHEN THE WATERS FLOODED MY EARS WITH KNOWING WHISPERS.
INVEST IN EVOLUTION REVERSE THE GENETIC CREDIT CRUNCH COMPOUND THE INTEREST OF BIODIVERSITY
...RE-WILD THE HUMAN MIND, GET PAST THIS DOMESTICATED CREATIVITY ... NO MORE iPODS, iPHONES, iHUMANS ... WE NEED TO REINVENT FIRE! IGNITE YOUR SAVAGE INTELLIGENCE ... PREPARE FOR THE MILLION YEAR PROFIT CYCLES...
THE APPLAUSE RESEMBLED A STAMPEDE OF NORTH AMERICAN BISON. I ALMOST PEED MY PANTS.
CLAP CLAP CLAP CLAP CLAP CLAP CLAP! CLAP CLAP CLAP CLAP CLAP CLAP CLAP CLAP CLAP CLAP CLAP CLAP
YOU'RE WELCOME...

WHAT'S YOUR BATHROOM LIKE? DO YOU LET IT GO... ALLOWING LAYERS OF GRIME AND SCENT TO ACCUMULATE UNTIL YOU'RE FORCED TO CAMOUFLAGE THEM WITH A CHEMICAL APPROXIMATION OF SPRING?
?
CONSIDER THE MODERN BATHROOM. WHAT LIES BEHIND THIS INJUNCTION TO CLEAN? HOW DID THIS ANTISEPTIC ROOM WHERE EXCREMENT MAGICALLY DISAPPEARS COME TO BE?
WHAT DO WE GAIN BY SEVERING THE CONNECTION BETWEEN OUR BOWELS AND THE FERTILITY CYCLES OF THE SOIL?
THE HUMAN GASTROINTESTINAL TRACT IS A MARVEL OF EVOLUTIONARY ENGINEERING. BEST OF ALL IT'S COPYRIGHT FREE... IMAGINE THAT!
HAVE YOU FOUND WHERE THE TRAIL LEADS? I THINK YOU ALREADY KNOW... I TRUST YOU'VE BEEN TAKING YOUR MEDICATION?
!
SLAM
I STOOD THERE FOR A LONG TIME, UNABLE TO GO.
SHIT!
IN THE POOL I WAS DISORIENTED. I HOVERED NEAR THE SURFACE UNABLE TO DECIDE WHETHER I WAS LOOKING UP AT THE CEILING OR DOWN INTO THE DEPTHS OF THE WATER.
I WAS NO LONGER SURE THAT THE WOMAN EXISTED IN THE SAME SPACE TIME CONTINUUM AS ME. COMMUNICATION BETWEN US WOULD BE IMPOSSIBLE WITHOUT SOME KIND OF INTER-DIMENSIONAL LEAP OF FAITH.
WHAT AM I WAITING FOR?

"YOUR PARTICIPATION IS NEEDED ON AN OFFSITE PROJECT..."

WE WERE ACCOMPANIED BY A COUPLE OF MEMBERS OF THE BRANDING TEAM, AND A PERSON I DIDN'T KNOW. LUBBOCK WAS CONSPICUOUSLY ABSENT.

WE ARRIVED AT ANOTHER CORPORATE CAMPUS AND ENTERED THE PREMISES SOMEWHAT OBLIQUELY. AT THIS POINT MY RECOLLECTION OF THE EVENTS THAT FOLLOWED BECOMES HAZY AT BEST...

"GO, GO!"

"IT REEKS OF ARTIFICIAL FERTILIZER..."

APPARENTLY THE PLACE BELONGED TO A FIRM THAT WAS RESISTING A TAKEOVER ATTEMPT BY OUR COMPANY.

"MEET KURZWEIL YOUR CEO."
"HI..., SIR..."
"NO TITLES!"

"WE'RE HERE TO STAKE OUR LEGITIMATE CLAIM... THE TAKEOVER HAS ALREADY HAPPENED, THEY JUST DON'T KNOW IT YET... THERE IS NO RESISTANCE TO HISTORICAL INEVITABILITY..."

"MMHMMHMMHM..."

"TONIGHT WE MAKE AN INVESTMENT TO FACILITATE THE RESTRUCTURING OF ANTIQUATED BUSINESS MODELS... WE COME TO FERTILIZE THIS BARREN SOIL WITH THE SEEDS OF OUR CORPORATE DNA..."

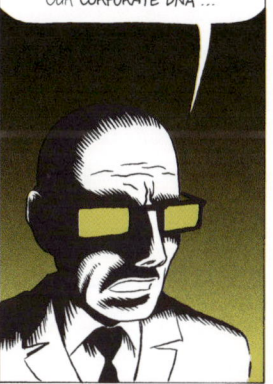

"ACTION PLAN: SHED YOUR CIVILIZED INHIBITIONS! DELIVERABLE: GARDEN OF PURE PROFIT... GOING FORWARD, COME THE PARADIGM SHIFT, EVOLUTIONARY SYNERGIES WILL COMPOUND..."

"AND THEN WE'LL RETURN TO REAP THE HARVEST..."

KURZWEIL MADE THE FIRST DEPOSIT... I REALIZED WHY THE BRANDING TEAM WAS CREATIVELY BLOCKED... CONSTIPATED BY OUTDATED MARKETING ASSUMPTIONS.

I WATCHED A SMALL GOLDEN STREAM FORM ON THE CONCRETE FLOWING AROUND MY FEET... I WAS THE HEADWATERS OF THE NILE... HERACLITUS IN THE EVERCHANGING RIVER...

A FAINT HUM OF ELECTRICAL ENGINE...

...SECURITY GUARD ON A SEGWAY...

"YOU FU--"

SPARK OF CREATION...

THUD

I DOVE EAGERLY INTO THE DEPTHS. AT THE BOTTOM SHE WAS WAITING FOR ME... THE CHANNEL WAS FINALLY WIDE OPEN...
WE COMMUNICATED NON-VERBALLY, LIKE TWO CELLS ENGAGING IN OSMOTIC FLUID EXCHANGE...
I COULDN'T HAVE BEEN OUT FOR LONG.
THE GUARD MUST HAVE GONE TO FIND THE OTHERS...
MY MOUTH WAS RAPIDLY FILLING WITH BLOOD.
I THINK HE BROKE A COUPLE OF TEETH...
THE RIGHT SIDE OF MY FACE PULSED WITH PAIN. I DREW A DEEP BREATH.
IT WAS A PRIMAL GESTURE, NOT PREMEDITATED OR PLANNED...
I STOOD THERE FOR A LONG TIME WATCHING
BLOOD CONGEAL INTO THE LOGO OF THE NEX
GREAT GLOBAL CORPORATION.

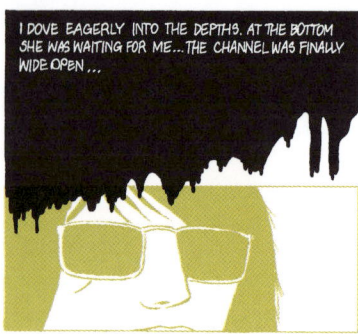

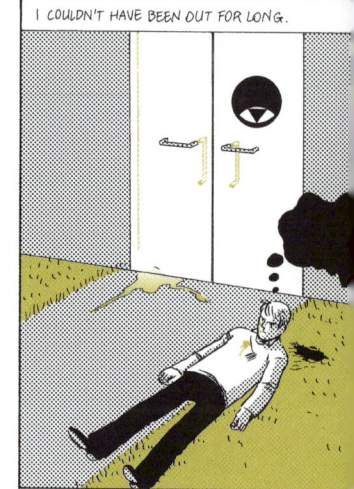

SPACE

– 100,000 MILES

– 10,000 Miles

PMS 021 ORANGE

COZY APOCALYPSE

First appearance: *MOME 21*, 2011

– 1,000 Miles

– 100 Miles

– 1 Mile

| 1,000,000,000 BC | 1,000,000 BC | 500,000 BC | 40,000 |

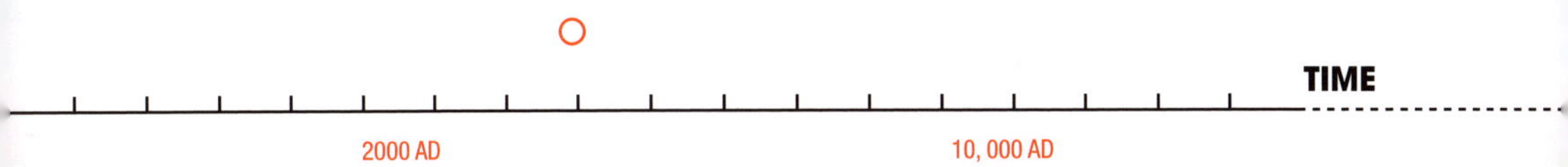
TIME
2000 AD
10, 000 AD

THE HOUSE WAS A DESPERATE INVESTMENT. THE ROOTLESS CITY LIFE BROUGHT OUR MARRIAGE TO THE BRINK OF DISASTER. LIFE IN THE SUBURBS SEEMED THE PERFECT ANTIDOTE.
WHHHR
I DIDN'T EXPECT THE PLACE TO REQUIRE SO MUCH WORK ...
WHEW !! HALF WAY DONE...
WHHHR
FROM THE START WE BECAME BESIEGED BY PLUMBERS, GARDENERS, WINDOW SALESMEN, ELECTRICIANS ...
WHHHRR
ELLO M'AM
WHY HELLO THERE
ALL OF THEM READY TO SERVICE OUR EVERY NEED...
I NEEDED SOMETHING TO OCCUPY MY WANDERING MIND...
HMM... THIS IS TOO TALL FOR THIS PUSH MOWER.
I HAD TO REASSERT CONTROL.
SHOULD I CALL THE PLUMBER?
NO!
DIDN'T YOU SAY YOU HATED MOWING ?
I DIDN'T LIKE THE WAY THE GARDNER OPERATED ...
WHAT ABOUT THIS THING?
IT'S SOME KIND OF FAST GROWING NATIVE PRAIRIE GRASS. I WAS GONNA WEED WHACK IT ...
LEAVE IT... I KINDA LIKE IT.
I WAS DETERMINED TO TURN THE HOUSE INTO THE NUCLEUS OF OUR NEW REALITY...

A FLOOD ADVISORY WAS ANNOUNCED TODAY ...
THINK THEY'RE RIGHT? IT'S REALLY TORRENTIAL OUT THERE... IT LOOKS LIKE A MONSOON!
GLOBAL WARMING IS HERE!
HAVE YOU SEEN THIS? A SCIENTIST CLAIMS THAT THE AMAZON RAINFOREST WAS ONCE A GARDEN!
WILD KINGDOM
I BETTER CHECK THE BASEMENT...
GET SOME OLD T-SHIRTS. WE CAN USE THEM AS RAGS IN CASE...
CRAP!
THE HOUSE BEGAN PAYING DIVIDENDS...
THESE ARE RAGS!? I REALLY LIKED THEM ON YOU...
THIS IS AN EMERGENCY...
WANT TO SEE MY NEW PAIR?
WE SPENT HOURS IN THE BASEMENT. OUTSIDE THE WORLD WAS TRANSFORMED.
THE MANICURED TURF PEELED AWAY REVEALING A SMALL GLIMPSE OF THE VAST OCEAN OF DISCONTENT BOILING BENEATH THE SURFACE.
LOOK, THERE'S MOLLY.
HI
?
BOOP
I JUST GOT FIRED VIA TEXT MESSAGE.

...E FLOOD WATERS ABATED WITHIN HOURS. A DAY LATER THE ...RKET CRASHED AND THE ECONOMY FELL OFF A CLIFF. THE ...OMPANY THAT FIRED ME WENT UP IN SMOKE.

THE REST OF THE WORLD CEASED TO EXIST...

"WHAT ARE ALL THESE WEIRD NEW PLANTS...?"

"JUST WEEDS"

"A MONARCH..."

WITHIN THE PERIMETER OF OUR FENCE A NEW REALITY WAS BEGINNING TO TAKE ROOT...

...WAITED... IN OUR SUBURBAN EDEN, FOR THE ...VITABLE COLLAPSE OF CIVILIZATION...

"WHY HADN'T THE LIGHTS GONE OUT YET?"

THE IMPENDING DOOM ACTED AS A POWERFUL APHRODISIAC. OUR TROUBLED PAST DISSOLVED IN THE CORROSIVE PHEROMONES OF THE UNCERTAIN FUTURE... ONLY THE PRESENT REMAINED... OVERFLOWING... OVERGROWN... SATURATED WITH THE ROMANCE OF DECAY.

BOOM

"WHAT WAS THAT?!"

...BURNING CAR WAS A REASSURING SIGN... ...FIRST CONCRETE MANIFESTATION OF THE ...ING INSURRECTION...

"IS THAT..."

THE TRUE NATURE OF THE CAR... UNLEASHED

"THAT'S OUR CAR!"

"NO..."

THE BLAZE ILLUMINATED THE PATH FORWARD... TOWARDS A BRIGHT NEW WORLD.

77

WHEN THE COP SHOWED UP I RESISTED THE URGE TO KILL HIM. I WAS SHOCKED THAT LAW ENFORCEMENT STILL FUNCTIONED...
SO... IT WAS JUST SOME JOY RIDING KIDS?
YAH ... YOU DIDN'T NOTICE THE CAR GO MISSING FOR A FEW DAYS?
UH... AND THEY JUST BLEW IT UP?
TO GET RID OF EVIDENCE... WHAT DID YOU SAY YOUR JOB WAS...? COMPUTERS?
I SUGGEST YOU MOW THIS JUNGLE...
UM...
FRANKLY, I'M SURPRISED THE CITY HASN'T DONE ANY-THING ABOUT IT YET!
THE CITY DID DO SOMETHING ABOUT IT... THE VERY NEXT DAY ORDER WAS RESTORED... WITH THE HELP OF GASOLINE POWERED LAWN EQUIPMENT.
THE FUTURE WAS DELAYED AGAIN. THE MARKETS RALLIED. CONSUMER CONFIDENCE REBOUNDED.
HAVE FUN AT YOUR PARENTS...
BYE!
BUT... LIKE A SCIENCE EXPERIMENT IT CAN BE REPRODUCED...
THERE ARE OTHER LABORATORIES TWEAKING... IMPROVING...
HELLO?
BETA TESTING THE NEXT APOCALYPSE
A NEW VENTURE?
IN HO CHI MINH CITY? I'LL TAKE THE NEXT FLIGHT OUT...
END

HOTEL SILENCIO
IE IDEA CAME TO JACOB JENAS WHILE TAYING AT A HOTEL UNDERGOING MAJOR ENOVATION.
THUD
BANG
BLAH, BLAH, BLAH, BLAH!
HAM
KLANG
WITHIN WEEKS A SUITABLE LOCATION WAS FOUND.
BOOM BOX
EACH ROOM WAS OUTFITTED WITH STATE OF THE ART SOUND PROOFING MATERIALS.
IE OPENING OF HOTEL SILENCIO MADE JACOB INTO A MINOR LEBRITY IN THE ACADEMIC WORLD.
THE SOLUTION TO 'NOISE POLLUTION' IS NOT EVASION BY ZONING, IT IS NEW GOODS AND SERVICES: NEW ACOUSTICAL MATERIALS, NEW EQUIPMENT, ETC.
XCESSIVE NOISE IS OT A PROBLEM OF OGRESS, BUT VIDENCE OF AGNATION!
ALL MANNER OF ANTI-NOISE DEVICES WENT INTO PRODUCTION.
EXPENSIVE EAR PLUGS WERE INTRODUCED AS FASHION ACCESSORIES.
LIBRARIES BECAME POPULAR DATING DESTINATIONS.
SILENT FILMS SAW A BRIEF RESURGENCE ON TV.
OCUMENTARY ABOUT MONKS UNDER VOW OF SILENCE BECAME A SURPRISE THAT SAME SUMMER.
BUT, IT SOON BECAME APPARENT THAT MOST GUESTS FOUND EXTREME SILENCE TO BE A DISCONCERTING EXPERIENCE.
WHAT WAS THAT!?
GURGLE
A FEW MONTHS LATER THE HOTEL WAS CONVERTED INTO A RECORDING STUDIO FOR AVANT GARDE MUSICIANS.
UH
STUDIO PIN DROP
HERE FOR THE RADIATOR SESSIONS? SECOND FLOOR, ROOM TWENTY SIX.
T. KACZYNSKI '08

SPACE

100,000 MILES

10,000 Miles

C 40
M 5
Y 10
K 5

MUSIC FOR NEANDERTHALS

First appearance: *MOME 22*, 2011

1,000 Miles

100 Miles

1 Mile

1,000,000,000 BC   1,000,000 BC   500,000 BC   40,000

○

|—|—|—|—|—|—|—|—|—|—|—|—|—|—|—|—| **TIME** - - - - - - - - - -
　　　2000 AD　　　　　　　　　　10, 000 AD

THIS IS A MUSICAL. IT'S ANTON AVANTI'S 9TH FILM.
BEFORE SHOOTING STARTED, THE CAST AND CREW WERE SUBJECTED TO CAVEMAN BOOT CAMP... FOR 18 MONTHS THEY FORMED A MICRO-SOCIETY DEDICATED TO LIVE AND LEARN LIKE EARLY HUMANS.
BACK TO PLANET EARTH
THIS IS ADAM MAXWELL. MUSICIAN TURNED ACTOR.
TOUCH AND SL__IDE
E'S NOT A VERY GOOD ACTOR, BUT HIS UNIQUE LARYNX
ND PHYSICAL ABILITY WON HIM A SPOT ON THIS FILM.
CRITICS DESCRIBED HIS MUSIC AS 'BEWILDERING...' 'NOISY' AND 'RANDOM NONSENSE.'
CRITICS AREN'T AWARE OF ADAM AS AN ACTOR.
ATRAK BORG!
CHE LIM!
HO!
MLAK MLAK DROOL
ZAYON!
A TY GWOOP!

THE CRACKLE OF BURNING TWIGS. MASTICATION. BREEZE. BREATHING. QUIET. AN AMBIENT SOUNDTRACK FORMS IN ADAM'S HEAD.

ADAM KNEW THE FIGHT WAS COMING. IT WAS IN THE SCRIPT... BUT IN THE MOMENT, KNOWING IT FELT... UNNATURAL... LIKE A PREMONITION OR PROPHECY. BUT HE KNEW HE'D REACT WITH TOTAL SURPRISE. 18 MONTHS OF PAVLOVIAN TRAINING WILL GENERATE THE CORRECT RESPONSE.

SCRATCH

SNIFF

IT WASN'T EXACTLY A SCREAM... SHRILL... PULSATING... ALMOST HUMAN...

EEEYOW

EEEYAH

HO! GORO!

OUF

OW...

YOU OK?

OH GOD! I'M SO SORRY!

86

OH MAN...
I THINK MY NOSE IS BROKEN...
WAS THAT A REAL ROCK?
I MUST'VE GRABBED THE WRONG ONE...
WHAT'S GOING ON?
DID YOU HEAR ADAM'S SCREAM?
YEAH... I ALMOST FROZE UP! ... SO... WHERE'S ANTON?
WE NEED A DOCTOR...
THE DULL SOUND OF THE ROCK HITTING HIS FACE ECHOED AROUND HIS SKULL.
IT TOOK A LONG TIME TO CONVINCE HIMSELF THAT HE WASN'T DREAMING...
THIS WAS THE FIRST TIME ADAM RETURNED HOME SINCE PRODUCTION BEGAN ON THE FILM.
SELECT
GET WELL SOON.
X
SELECT
HOW WAS THE SURGERY?
X
SELECT
BRUNCH? CAFE BUFFON. ONE HOUR.
REPLY
OK. CU.
SEND
HOW QUICKLY EVERYDAY RITUALS BECOME STRANGE AND MANNERED...
THE CITY SOUNDED... CHEAP... TINNY CELL PHONE SPEAKERS... CAR HORNS... THE EFFECT IS CUMULATIVE... LIKE MERCURY POISONING... TOXIC... INTOXICATING...

WHILE WALKING, HIS BODY CONTORTS... IT'S MORE COMFORTABLE IN A PRE-HISTORIC CONFIGURATION...
THE PEDESTRIAN DIN IS WEIRDLY SYNCHRONIZED...
LIKE A MARCHING ARMY... HYPNOTIC ... CIVILIZING...
UTENSILS ON PLATES. SOFT MUZAK. CONVERSATION. FIZZ OF CARBONATED WATER. AWKWARD SILENCES.
I TOLD YOU NOT TO DO THIS FILM!
YOUR BEAUTIFUL NOSE...
ARNOLD SZYNBERG ADAM'S AGENT.
IT'S NOT THAT BAD...
NOT THAT BAD!? YOU HAVE A BROKEN NOSE!
IT'S NOT BROKEN JUST SPRAINED...
SPRAINED ※ TSK... DON'T MAKE FUN OF ME, ADAM... I'M JUST MORE THAN A LITTLE CONCERNED ABOUT THIS PICTURE...
BUT...
MAY I...?
IT'S OVER BUDGET... OVER TIME... THERE ARE TOO MANY ACCIDENTS. IT'S ABOUT SINGING CAVEMEN...
I KNOW THAT...
I CAN TELL WHEN A FILM IS IN SERIOUS TROUBLE...

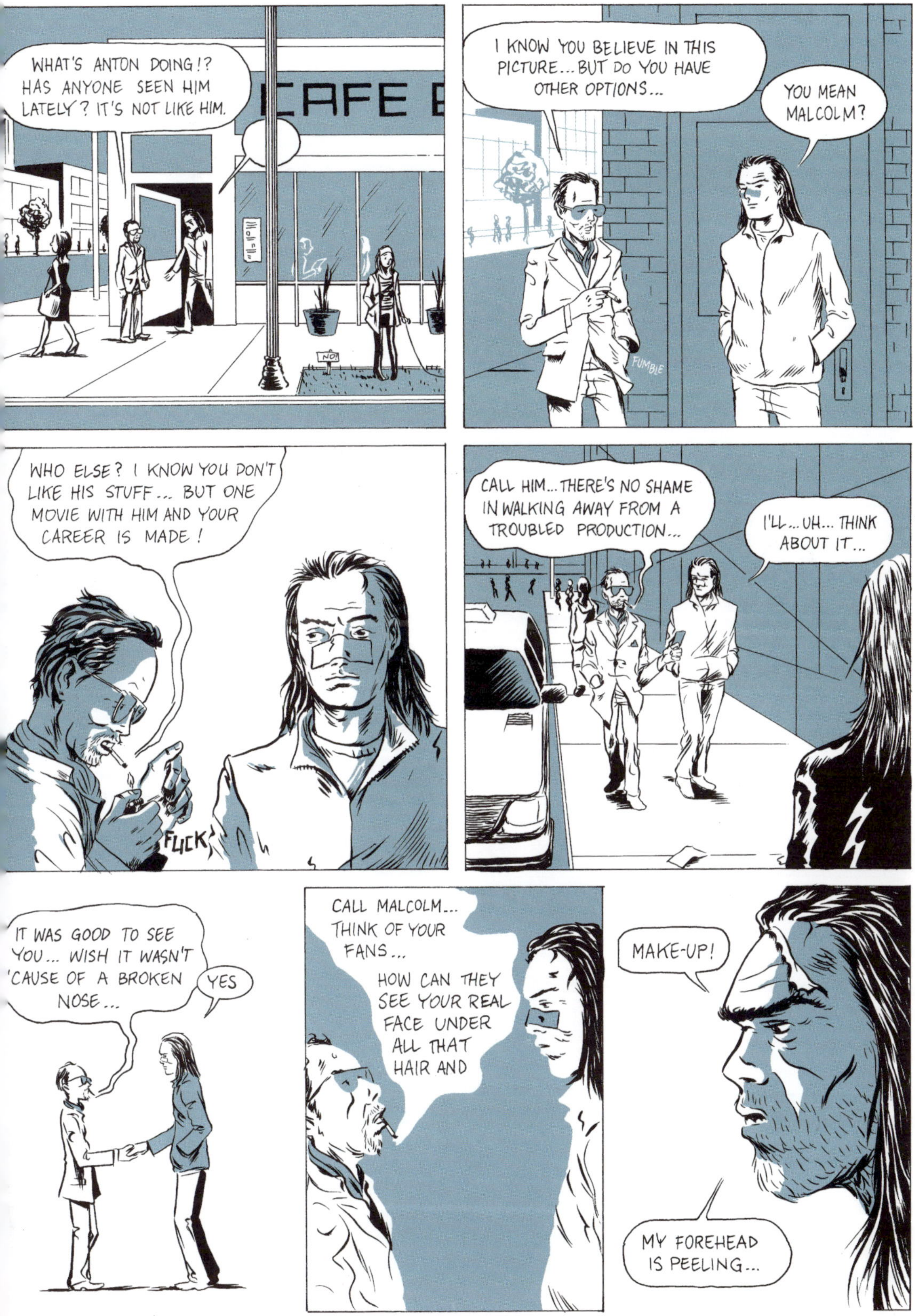
WHAT'S ANTON DOING!? HAS ANYONE SEEN HIM LATELY? IT'S NOT LIKE HIM.
CAFE
NO!
I KNOW YOU BELIEVE IN THIS PICTURE... BUT DO YOU HAVE OTHER OPTIONS...
YOU MEAN MALCOLM?
FUMBLE
WHO ELSE? I KNOW YOU DON'T LIKE HIS STUFF... BUT ONE MOVIE WITH HIM AND YOUR CAREER IS MADE!
FUCK
CALL HIM... THERE'S NO SHAME IN WALKING AWAY FROM A TROUBLED PRODUCTION...
I'LL... UH... THINK ABOUT IT...
IT WAS GOOD TO SEE YOU... WISH IT WASN'T 'CAUSE OF A BROKEN NOSE...
YES
CALL MALCOLM... THINK OF YOUR FANS...
HOW CAN THEY SEE YOUR REAL FACE UNDER ALL THAT HAIR AND
MAKE-UP!
MY FOREHEAD IS PEELING...

HEADPHONES ... FOR ADAM THIS IS MANKINDS GREATEST INVENTION...
SO I HEARD SOME WEIRD STUFF ABOUT ANTON ...
YEAH...?
THEY STIFLE THE RHYTHMS OF EVERY-DAY... THEY TRANSFORM THE WORLD. A PRIVATE UNIVERSE IN YOUR HEAD.
ADAM
SNARL
DID ADAM JUST SNARL? WHAT IS HE LISTENING TO?
ANTON WANTS YOU.
?
AND TELL HIM I'M THE KEY GRIP NOT A GOPHER!
ANTON?
HAVE YOU BEEN HIDING IN A CAVE?
HEH!
MAXWELL... LISTEN I'M SORRY ABOUT YOUR NOSE...
AH FORGET IT... IT WAS JUST AN ACCIDENT. ALL IN THE LINE OF DUTY...
I TOLD MARK TO THROW A REAL ROCK...
ITCH
YOU WHAT...?
LISTEN...
GAH...!
LOOK... I'M SORRY MAXWELL! THERE WAS NO ILL INTENT... OK? I HAVE TO TALK TO YOU ABOUT SOMETHING. I'VE BEEN IN THE CAVE LISTENING TO YOUR WORK... I THINK YOU CAN HELP US...

BY THE END OF THIS CONVERSATION, ADAM COMPLETELY FORGOT THE ROCK INCIDENT
MY WORK?
YOUR MUSIC. WE'VE BEEN TINKERING WITH THE CAVE'S ACOUSTICS...
WAIT, WHAT CAVE?
PAY ATTENTION, MAXWELL! THIS IS A CAVEMAN MOVIE. OF COURSE WE HAVE A CAVE...
I NEED SOMEONE WITH YOUR MUSICAL ABILITY
TO STAGE UNUSUAL AUDIO... ER, EXPERIENCES...
ANTON BROKE YOUR NOSE!?
WELL... TECHNICALLY, NO... MARK...
BUT HE ORCHESTRATED IT, RIGHT!?
YEAH...
I THINK HE JUST WANTED TO SHAKE US UP A LITTLE...
BY BREAKING YOUR NOSE?
HE'S SHAKING THE WHOLE MOVIE APART!
BUT IT'S GETTING INTERESTING... WE'RE BUILDING THIS CAVE... I'M HELPING HIM WITH SOME SOUND IDEAS...
YOU MEAN UNSOUND... HE'S A TYRANT!
ALL DIRECTORS ARE TYRANTS...
BUT MALCOLM... HE'S MORE OF AN... ENLIGHTENED... MONARCH. I THINK YOU'D LIKE HIS NEW FILM. IT'S ABOUT SOME FUTURISTIC SOCIETY...
SOUNDS OK...
HIS OFFER WON'T BE AROUND FOR LONG...
I KNOW... I JUST... I HAVE TO STAY HERE...

AN ARCHEOACOUSTICS EXPERT EXPLAINED THAT CAVES PICKED BY EARLY HUMANS WERE ACOUSTICALLY SIGNIFICANT.
WE DON'T HAVE THE BUDGET TO BUILD OUT OF ROCK... A SIMULATION WILL DO...
WHY NOT DO IT IN POST?
CERTAIN STALAGMITES AND STALACTITES HAD MUSICAL PROPERTIES. THE CAVE COULD BE PLAYED LIKE AN INSTRUMENT.
THIS MUST COST A FORTUNE!
SNORT
I WANT THE CAST TO FEEL THE REAL THING
MOST WALLS WITH ANCIENT ART EXHIBIT UNUSUAL ACOUSTIC PROPERTIES.
THE CAVE WAS MORE THAN A SHELTER. IT WAS MANKIND'S FIRST COMPLETE ENVIRONMENT... WITH CONTROL OVER LIGHTING, DECOR, AND SOUND.
ALMOST...
DUM
THE FIRST HUMANS ENTERED THE CAVES NO BETTER THAN THEIR LESS EVOLVED NEANDERTHAL COUSINS.
HELLO!
WHEN THEY EMERGED... 200,000 YEARS LATER, THEY WERE ... US...
HELLO
OLLEH
HELL

ONCE THE CAVE WAS FINISHED, THE SHOOTING SCHEDULE ACCELERATED.

EVEN THOUGH ADAM DESIGNED EVERY EFFECT THE POWER OF THE SOUND STILL SHOCKED HIM.

THE CAVE MIRRORED THE INSIDE OF HIS SKULL... HIS BODY, HIS BONES, HIS DNA VIBRATED... RESONATED... SHAKING OUT OBSOLETE GENES AND DEAD-END GENOMES.

HE SAW THE TERRIFYING SYNESTHETIC VISIONS THAT HOMO SAPIENS PREPARED FOR THE MUSICAL AND EMOTIONAL NEANDERTHALS.

FIRE CONQUERED THE COLD AND THE NIGHT. IN THE CAVE, MAN CONQUERED THE SOUL.

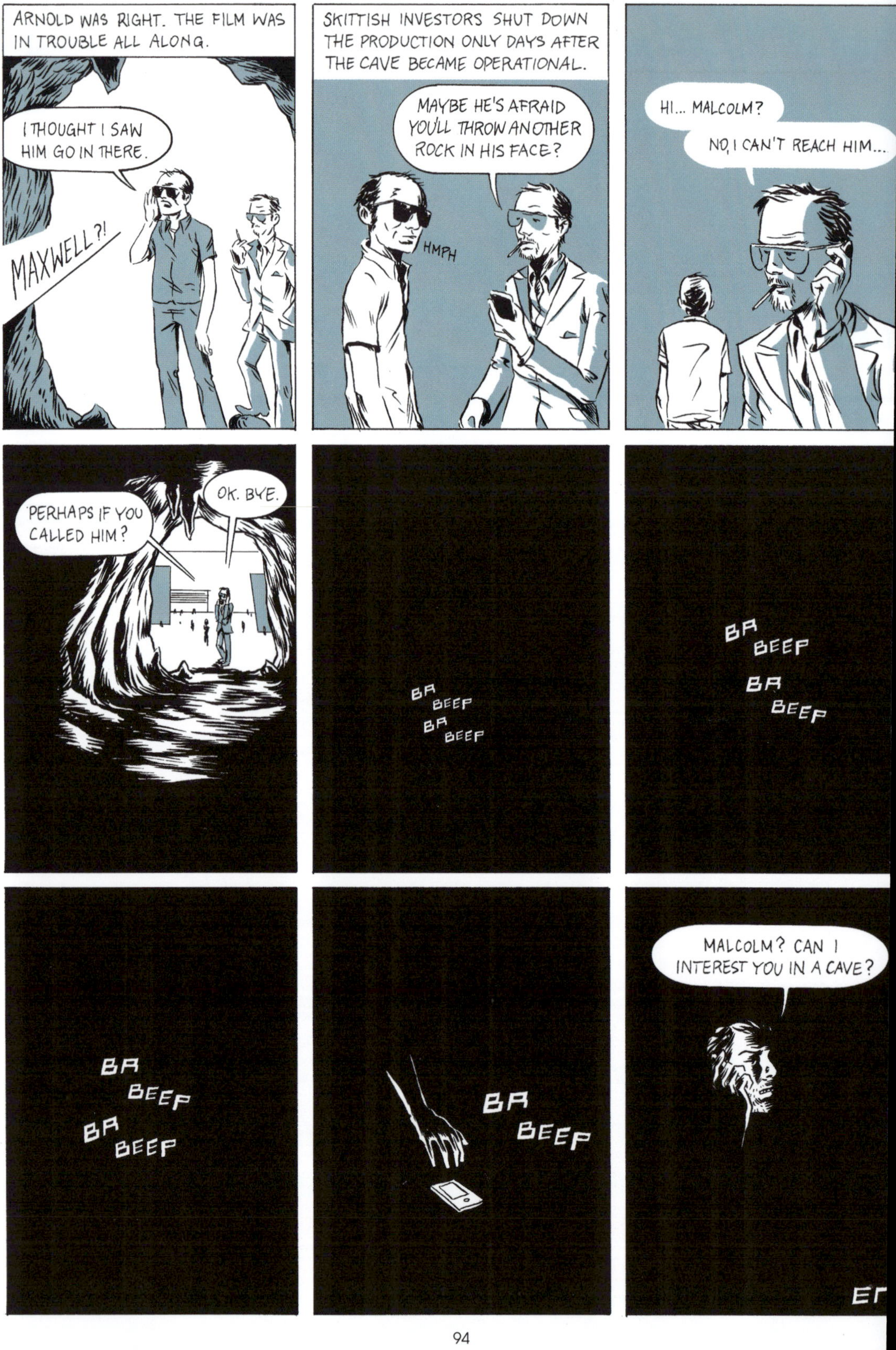

ARNOLD WAS RIGHT. THE FILM WAS IN TROUBLE ALL ALONG.
I THOUGHT I SAW HIM GO IN THERE.
MAXWELL?!
SKITTISH INVESTORS SHUT DOWN THE PRODUCTION ONLY DAYS AFTER THE CAVE BECAME OPERATIONAL.
MAYBE HE'S AFRAID YOU'LL THROW ANOTHER ROCK IN HIS FACE?
HMPH
HI... MALCOLM?
NO, I CAN'T REACH HIM...
PERHAPS IF YOU CALLED HIM?
OK. BYE.
BA BEEP BA BEEP
BA BEEP BA BEEP
BA BEEP BA BEEP
BA BEEP
MALCOLM? CAN I INTEREST YOU IN A CAVE?

SPACE

100,000 MILES

10,000 Miles

C 0
M 60
Y 80
K 0

THE NEW

First appearance: *Beta Testing the Apocalypse,* 2012

1,000 Miles

100 Miles

1 Mile

1,000,000,000 BC   1,000,000 BC   500,000 BC   40,000

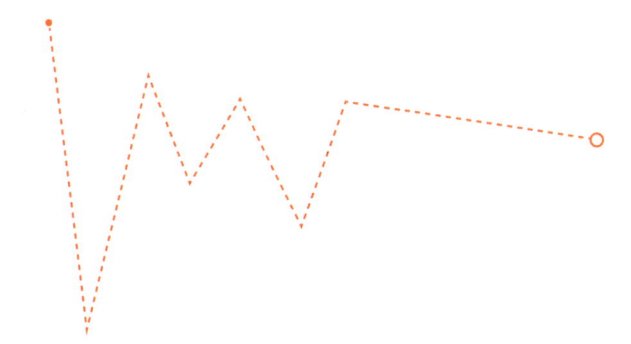

2000 AD   10,000 AD   **TIME**

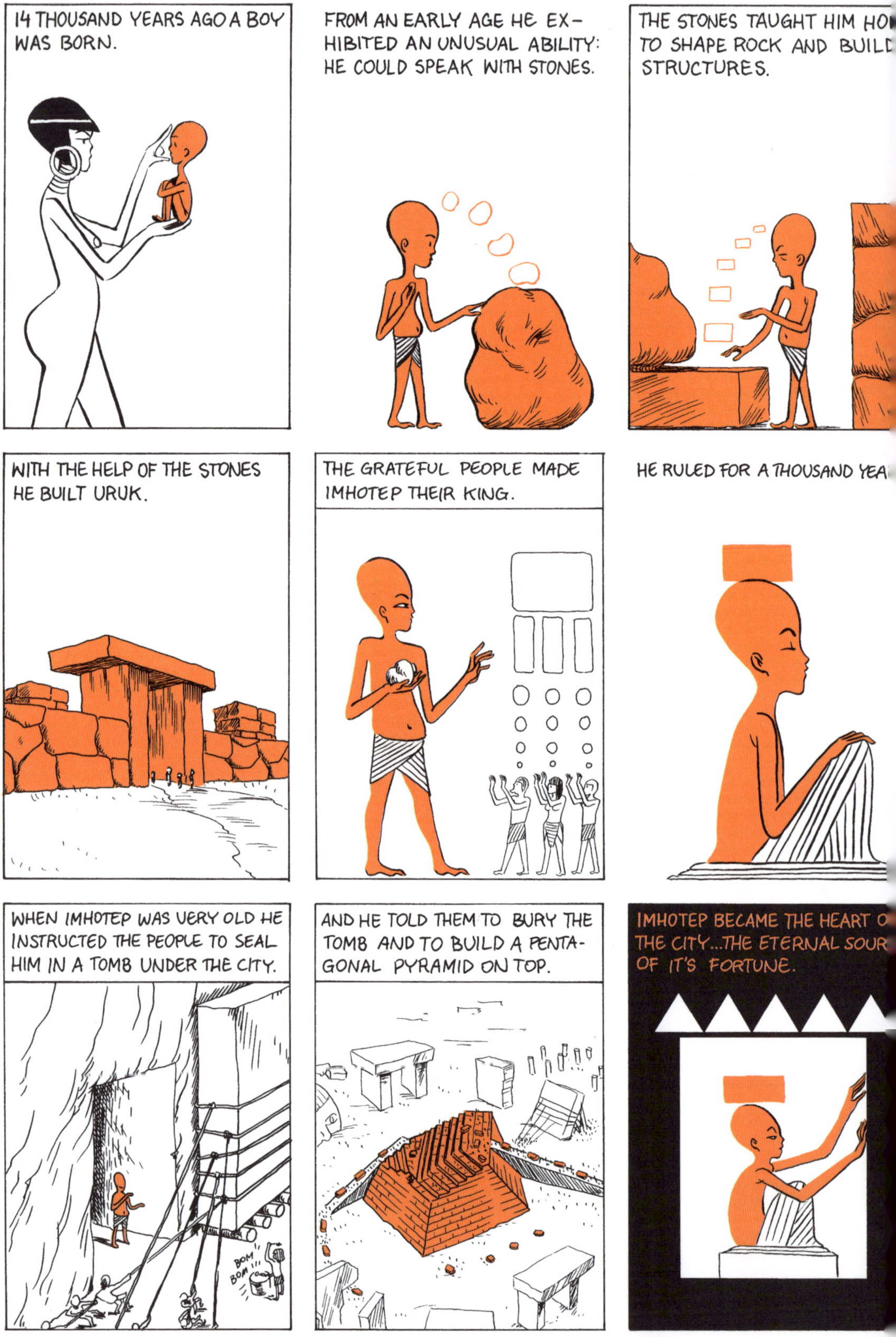

14 THOUSAND YEARS AGO A BOY WAS BORN.	FROM AN EARLY AGE HE EXHIBITED AN UNUSUAL ABILITY: HE COULD SPEAK WITH STONES.	THE STONES TAUGHT HIM HO[W] TO SHAPE ROCK AND BUIL[D] STRUCTURES.
WITH THE HELP OF THE STONES HE BUILT URUK.	THE GRATEFUL PEOPLE MADE IMHOTEP THEIR KING.	HE RULED FOR A THOUSAND YEA[RS]
WHEN IMHOTEP WAS VERY OLD HE INSTRUCTED THE PEOPLE TO SEAL HIM IN A TOMB UNDER THE CITY.	AND HE TOLD THEM TO BURY THE TOMB AND TO BUILD A PENTAGONAL PYRAMID ON TOP.	IMHOTEP BECAME THE HEART O[F] THE CITY...THE ETERNAL SOUR[CE] OF IT'S FORTUNE.

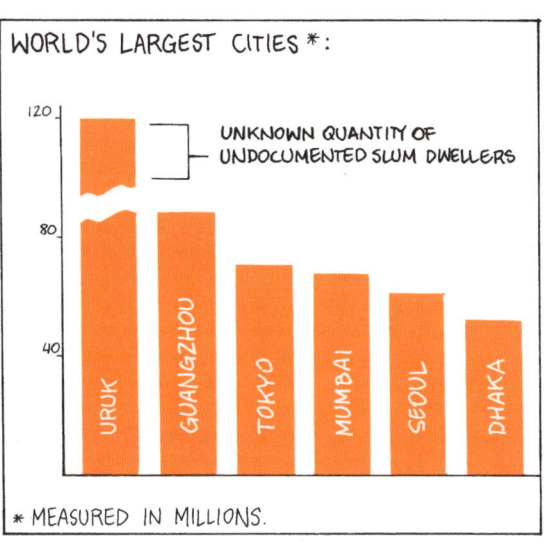

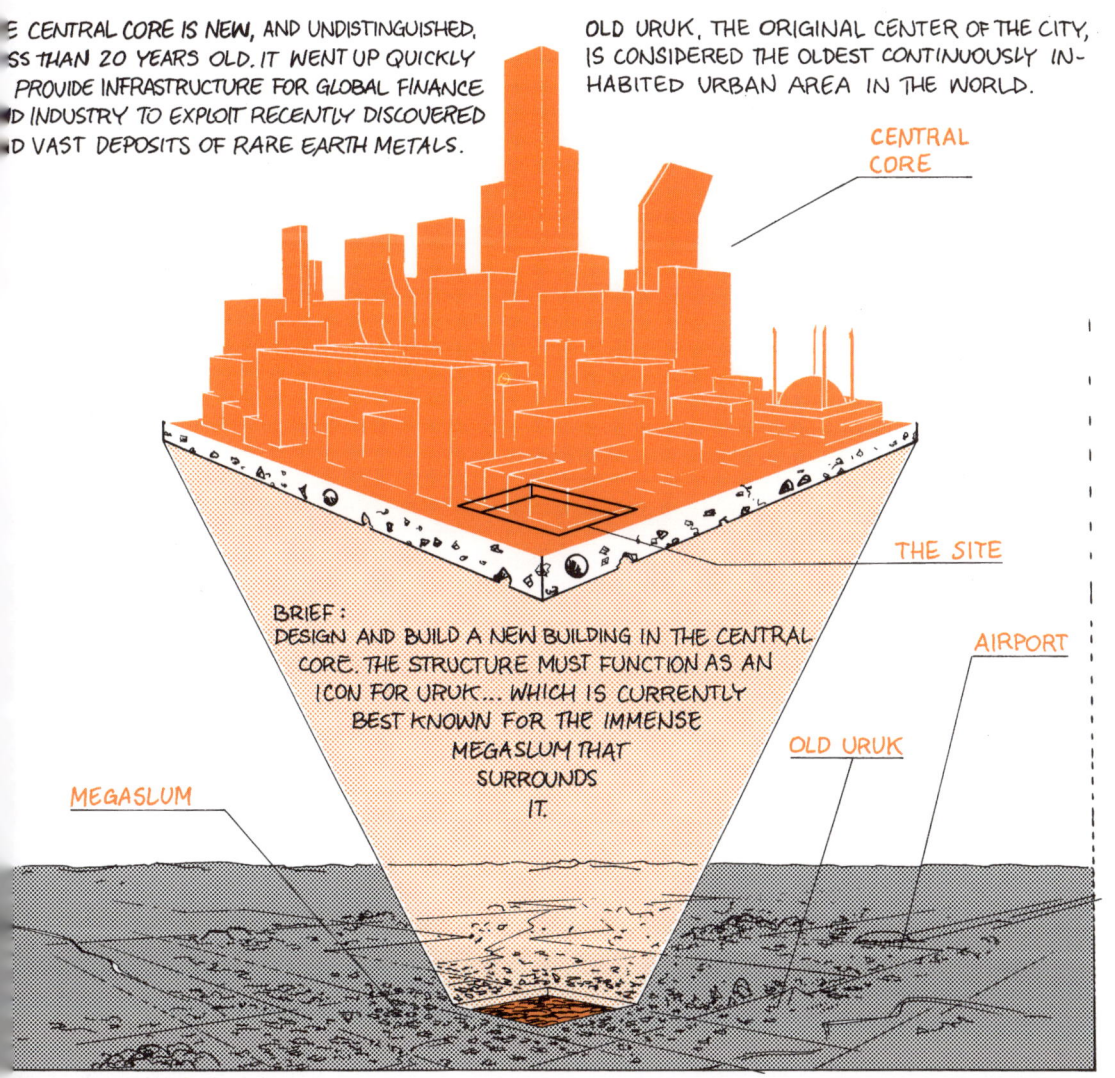

[MY] TEAM HAS BEEN STUDYING URUK FOR [S]EVERAL MONTHS.

WORLD'S LARGEST CITIES *:

UNKNOWN QUANTITY OF UNDOCUMENTED SLUM DWELLERS

URUK / GUANGZHOU / TOKYO / MUMBAI / SEOUL / DHAKA

* MEASURED IN MILLIONS.

[THE] CENTRAL CORE IS NEW, AND UNDISTINGUISHED, [LE]SS THAN 20 YEARS OLD. IT WENT UP QUICKLY [TO] PROVIDE INFRASTRUCTURE FOR GLOBAL FINANCE [AN]D INDUSTRY TO EXPLOIT RECENTLY DISCOVERED [AN]D VAST DEPOSITS OF RARE EARTH METALS.

OLD URUK, THE ORIGINAL CENTER OF THE CITY, IS CONSIDERED THE OLDEST CONTINUOUSLY INHABITED URBAN AREA IN THE WORLD.

CENTRAL CORE

THE SITE

BRIEF:
DESIGN AND BUILD A NEW BUILDING IN THE CENTRAL CORE. THE STRUCTURE MUST FUNCTION AS AN ICON FOR URUK... WHICH IS CURRENTLY BEST KNOWN FOR THE IMMENSE MEGASLUM THAT SURROUNDS IT.

AIRPORT

OLD URUK

MEGASLUM

THE BRUTAL VITALITY OF THE MEGASLUM IS PALPABLE EVEN FROM THE HELICOPTER.

UNDERNEATH THE DESPERATE CIRCUMSTANCES AND THE LAWLESS DARWINIAN STRUGGLE, A BARELY REPRESSED FERAL AMBITION IS READY TO BOIL OVER.

IN A WAY THE DISPOSSESSED ALREADY BUILT THE PERFECT MONUMENT TO URUK'S ENTRY INTO GLOBAL CAPITAL'S BUBBLE ECONOMY.

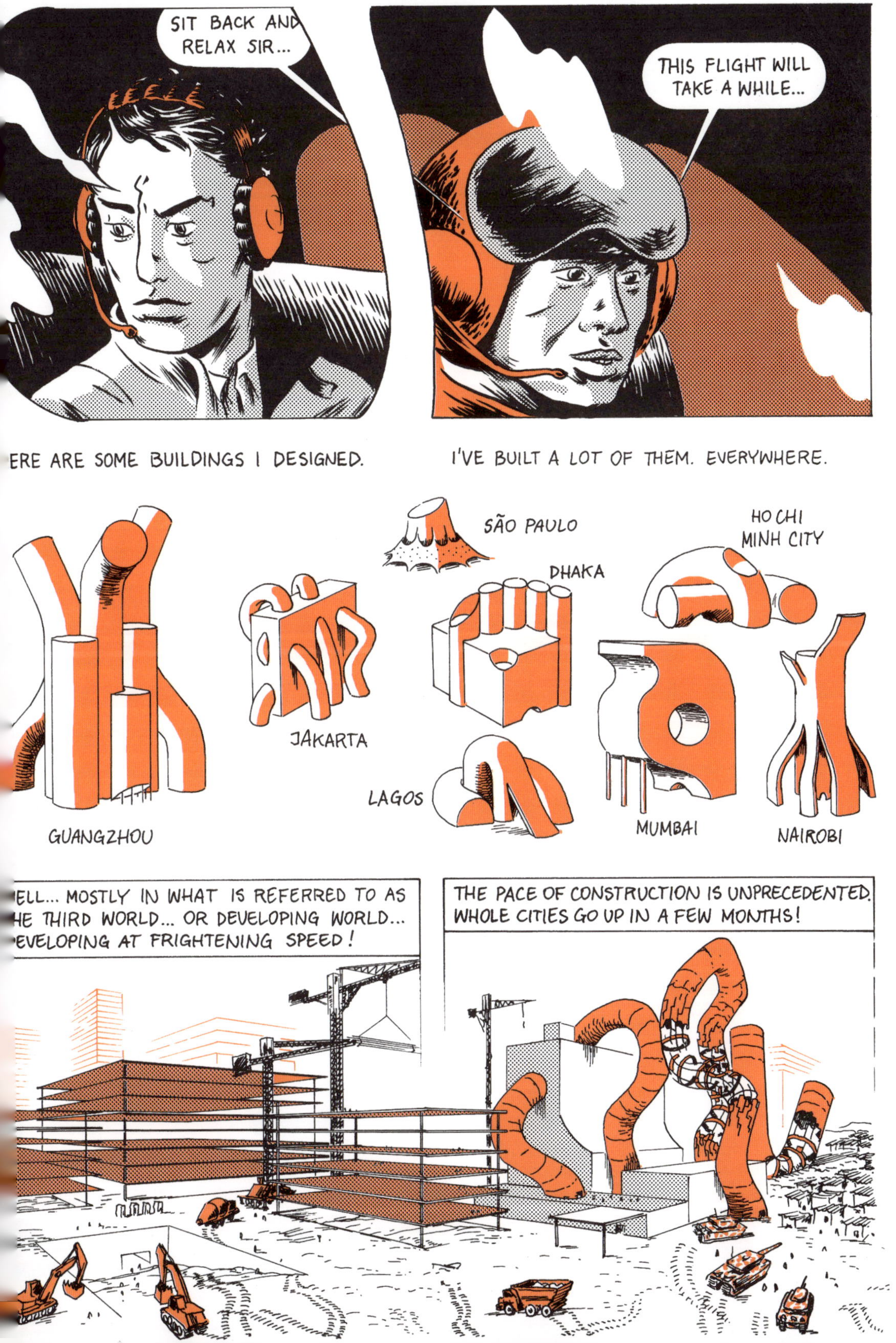

SIT BACK AND RELAX SIR...
THIS FLIGHT WILL TAKE A WHILE...
ERE ARE SOME BUILDINGS I DESIGNED.
I'VE BUILT A LOT OF THEM. EVERYWHERE.
GUANGZHOU
JAKARTA
SÃO PAULO
DHAKA
HO CHI MINH CITY
LAGOS
MUMBAI
NAIROBI
ELL... MOSTLY IN WHAT IS REFERRED TO AS HE THIRD WORLD... OR DEVELOPING WORLD... EVELOPING AT FRIGHTENING SPEED!
THE PACE OF CONSTRUCTION IS UNPRECEDENTED. WHOLE CITIES GO UP IN A FEW MONTHS!

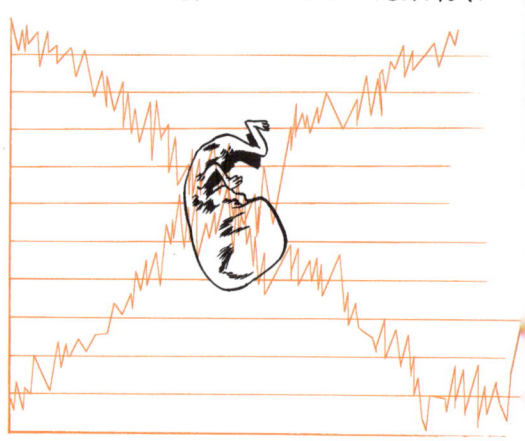

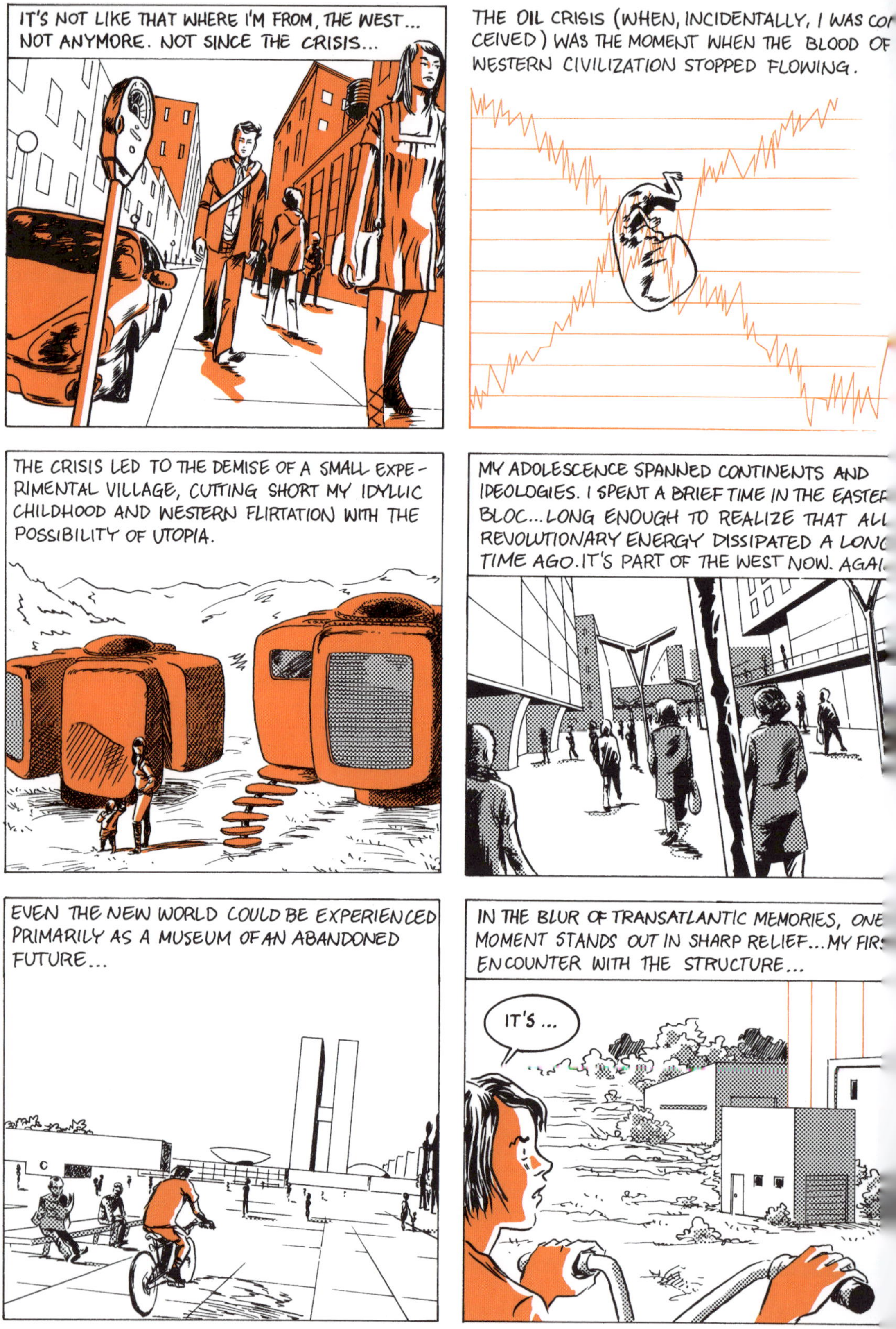

IT'S NOT LIKE THAT WHERE I'M FROM, THE WEST... NOT ANYMORE. NOT SINCE THE CRISIS...	THE OIL CRISIS (WHEN, INCIDENTALLY, I WAS CONCEIVED) WAS THE MOMENT WHEN THE BLOOD OF WESTERN CIVILIZATION STOPPED FLOWING.
THE CRISIS LED TO THE DEMISE OF A SMALL EXPERIMENTAL VILLAGE, CUTTING SHORT MY IDYLLIC CHILDHOOD AND WESTERN FLIRTATION WITH THE POSSIBILITY OF UTOPIA.	MY ADOLESCENCE SPANNED CONTINENTS AND IDEOLOGIES. I SPENT A BRIEF TIME IN THE EASTERN BLOC...LONG ENOUGH TO REALIZE THAT ALL REVOLUTIONARY ENERGY DISSIPATED A LONG TIME AGO. IT'S PART OF THE WEST NOW. AGAIN.
EVEN THE NEW WORLD COULD BE EXPERIENCED PRIMARILY AS A MUSEUM OF AN ABANDONED FUTURE...	IN THE BLUR OF TRANSATLANTIC MEMORIES, ONE MOMENT STANDS OUT IN SHARP RELIEF... MY FIRST ENCOUNTER WITH THE STRUCTURE...

"IT'S..."

I CALL IT THE STRUCTURE... IT WAS A MASSIVE GRAIN SILO...
UTILITARIAN, A SEED OF MODERNIST ARCHITECTURE
IMPOSSIBLY ANCIENT, ALMOST GEOLOGY
FROZEN IN SPACE...
OCCASIONALLY WE STUMBLE
ON THE CORRECT VANTAGE POINT,
THE RIGHT ANGLE... A PARALLAX SHIFT
OPENS LINES OF COMMUNICATION
AN INKLING OF SOMETHING
LARGER... GEOMETRIC ECHO
OF THE SILO REPEATING
WITHOUT DECAY
IN MY MIND.

SOMETHING WAS THERE,
HIDDEN IN THE DATA
SOMETHING EXTRA
AN EXCESS
AN UNNAMABLE
DISTANT INTERIOR...

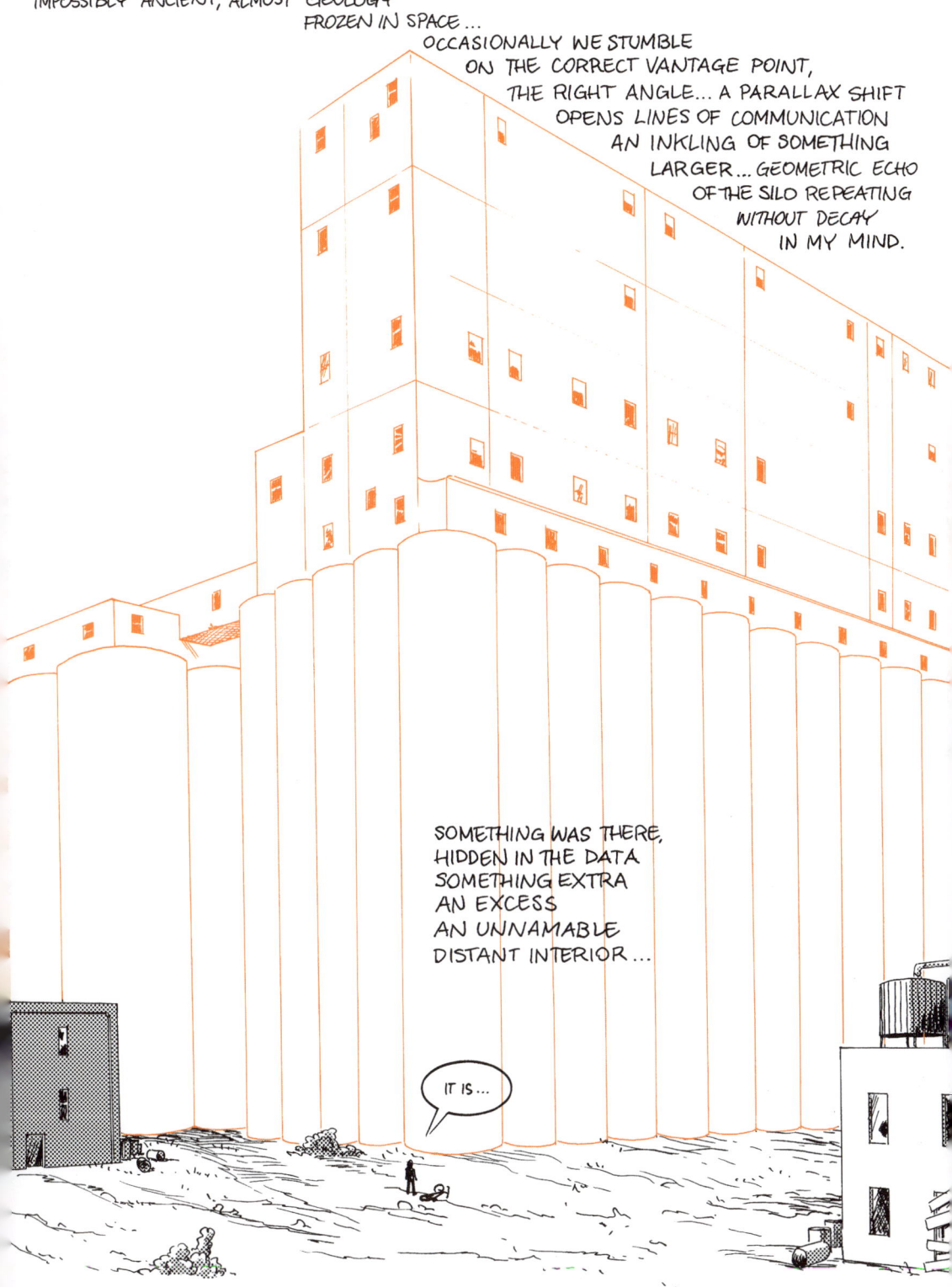

IT IS...

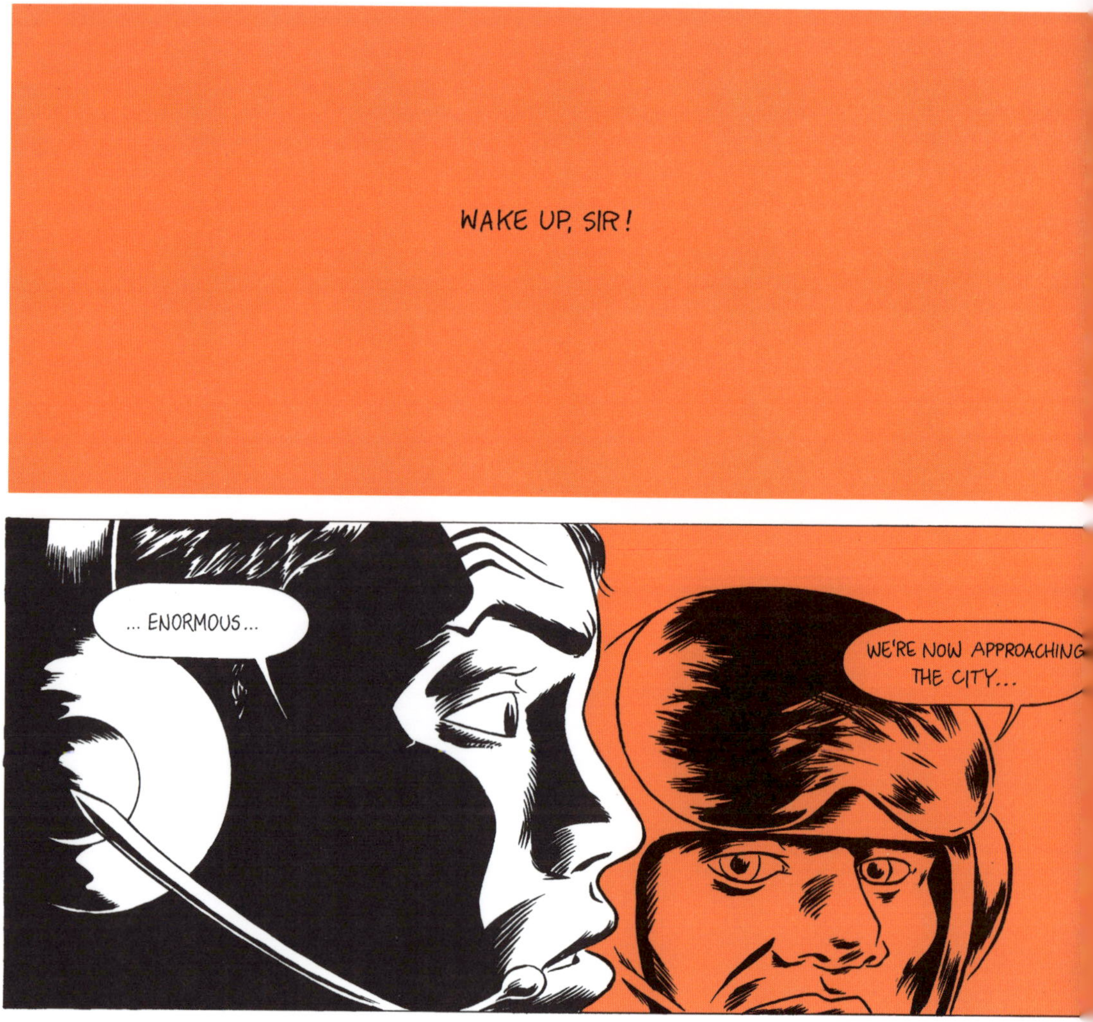
WAKE UP, SIR!
... ENORMOUS...
WE'RE NOW APPROACHING THE CITY...

REQUEST PERMISSI
TO ENTER CORE
AIR SPACE...
PPROACHING THE CITY? WHAT DO YOU
LL THIS MIASMIC URBAN FALLOUT
MANATING FROM THE CENTRAL CORE?
EXCUSE ME... MUST BE THE JETLAG...
ENDLESS DISTRICTS, CONSTRUCTED OUT OF TRASH, POWERED BY BLOOD, SWEAT, AND DISCARDED LITHIUM ION BATTERIES.

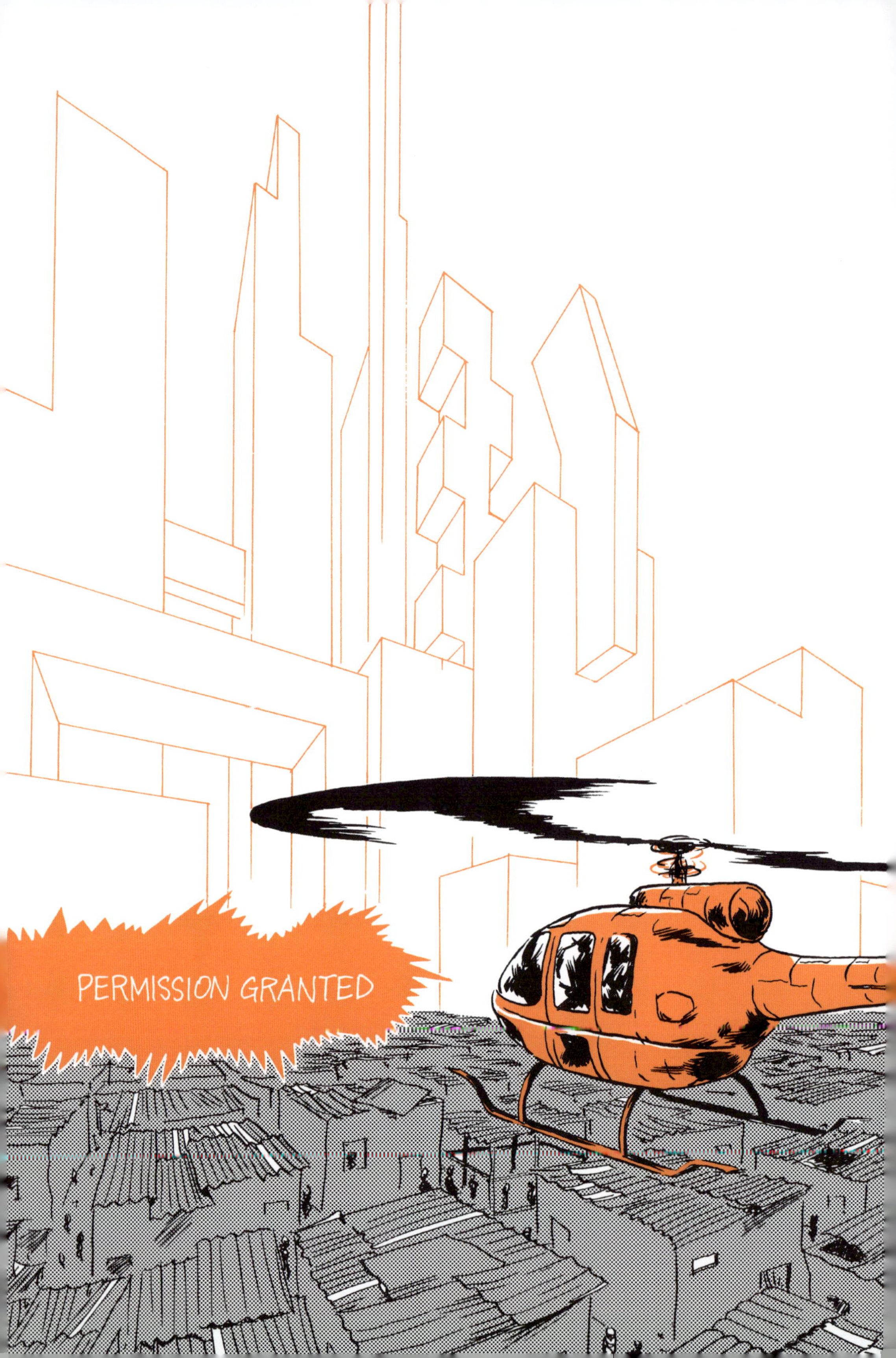
PERMISSION GRANTED

THE HELICOPTER TURNED SLIGHTLY AND
FOR A MOMENT
THE CENTRAL CORE OF
URUK REVEALED
ITS SINISTER GEOMETRY.

THE SLUMS DESPERATELY CIRCLED
THE INVISIBLE PERIMETER
MOTH-LIKE
FEEDING ON
EMPTY LUMINESCENCE.

WHOOP WHOOP WHOOP WHOOP WHOOP
WHOOP WHOOP WH
WHO
WELCOME MR. ______
HOW WAS YOUR FLIGHT?
MEMORABLE... AND OVERWHELMING...
WHO
WHOOP WHOOP WHOOP
DID YOU GET TO SEE OLD URUK AND THE FIVE SIDED PYRAMID?
NO...
TOO BAD. I'M SURE WE CAN ARRANGE A MORE INTIMATE VISIT.

THE KING IS EAGER TO SEE YOUR IDEAS. HE FEELS YOU CAN DO MUCH TO RESTORE URUK'S STATURE.
BUT YOU DON'T THINK SO?
FRANKLY, NO... WE ARE THE CHILDREN OF THE GREAT IMHOTEP, WORLD'S FIRST ARCHITECT... WE SHOULD BE THE ONES CREATING OUR ICONS...
FORGIVE ME... I TRUST THE KING, BUT...
OF COURSE.
THE NATIVES ARE ALWAYS DIFFICULT. IT'S IMPOSSIBLE FOR THEM TO STEP BACK AND SEE THE TRUE NATURE OF THE CITY. THE BELLY OF THE LEVIATHAN FEELS LIKE HOME...
CH BUILDING IS A MARKET HIGH, EACH STREET THE CHANNEL OF A FORGOTTEN RIVER, EVERY CITY NGEALS OUT OF GLOBAL CAPITAL FLOWS. PAST BOOMS AND BUSTS FORM ITS CALCIFIED SKYLINE.
MR. ______ TO SEE HIS MAJESTY.
E MOMENT
HASI?
______?!

WE MET IN CHANDIGARH, DURING AN ARCHITECTURAL COMPETITION. SHE ACCOMPANIED A MIDDLE EASTERN OIL MINISTER INTERESTED IN MY IDEAS.
PLEASE JOIN US FOR TEA IN MY TENT AFTER THE EVENT IS OVER...
IDEAS WERE ALL I HAD BACK THEN. I HAD YET T
BUILD A SINGLE PROJECT.
...THEIR STRENGTH IS THEIR SOFTNESS...
...THEY MELT INTO THE ENVIRONMEN ADAPTING TO IT.. AWARE OF THE SU ROUNDING CONTE
THE 'TENT' TURNED OUT TO BE AN IMPRESSIVE INFLATABLE MOBILE STRUCTURE... DESIGNED BY HASI.
WOW!
...WHOM I MISTOOK FOR A SERVANT...BUT BEFOR THE MINISTER PASSED OUT, WE WERE ALREADY A CUPS OF TEA INTO ARCHITECTURAL DELIGHTS.
EXCUSE ME
HIC
MORE INSAM CHA?
PLEASE! IT' DELICIOUS
WALKING CITIES, LE CORBUSIER, UTOPIAS, LOST WORLDS, TATLIN, POLIPHILO'S DREAM, THEORY OF THE DÉRIVE...
PLEASE TAKE MY CARD...
HEART
AT THE END OF THE NIGHT HER BUSINESS CARD THE MOST UNUSUAL TEXTURE..
HASI PARK
ARCHITECT

AAAAARGH!
WE BRIEFLY WORKED TOGETHER. I ADMIRED HER ASIAN VITALITY. SHE WAS ATTRACTED TO WESTERN IDEAS. WE THRIVED ON MUTUAL ORIENTALISM.
BUT IT COULDN'T LAST. SHE WAS ALREADY TOO WESTERN, TOO BRASH, TOO ROCK 'N ROLL...
SI WANTED TO REVIVE THE ABANDONED PROJECTS
WESTERN AVANT GARDES. A NOBLE EFFORT...
ISTEN UP!
WE'RE BUILDING A PARTICLE ACCELERATOR!
CONSTRUCTIVISM, FUTURISM, SITUATIONISM, POST-MODERNISM... BRILLIANT PERFORMANCES ALL.
AN ATOM SMASHER!
T HER VITALITY ONLY FURTHER EXPOSED THE
AUSTED WESTERN MODELS.
CLAP
SMASH!
CLAP
BACK TO WORK!
WOOP!
WE COMPLETED ONE BUILDING TOGETHER. IN MOSCOW. SHE RUTHLESSLY DECONSTRUCTED MY CONTRIBUTION. MY NEXT PROJECT WAS IN JAKARTA. HERS WAS IN LONDON.

WHAT THE FUCK ARE YOU DOING HERE !?
WORKING ON ANOTHER ICONIC PROJECT? YOU'RE GETTING REPETITIVE. SOMEONE SHOULD ALERT HIS MAJESTY.
PLEASE, MS. PARK...
I SHOULD'VE KNOWN HASI WOULD BE HERE.
...I CAN'T TOLERATE SUCH INSO ...
BAH! SPARE ME! JUST MAKE SURE HE DOES SOMETHING NEW AND INTERESTING.
SHE IS QUITE DIFFICULT...
WHATEVER PROJECT SHE IS WORKING ON WILL BE MAGNIFICEN
HOLD HIS FEET TO THE FIRE. HE PERFORMS BETTER UNDER DURESS. IF HE'S NOT WORKING OUT THERE MIGHT BE A LITTLE ROOM ON MY PROJECT... SAY HELLO TO THE KING!
FIRE BURNS COTTON STUPIDLY, PAYING NO HEED TO ITS PROPERTIES. FIRE INTERACTS WITH THE COTTON ONLY INSOFAR AS IT IS FLAMMABLE.
EXCUSE ME, SIR. HIS MAJESTY IS READY TO RECEIVE HIS GUEST.
THANK YOU.

I WILL WAIT FOR YOU HERE.
THANK YOU.
ENTER.
ER...
YOUR MAJESTY?
AH!
...Y...
YOU'RE HERE!

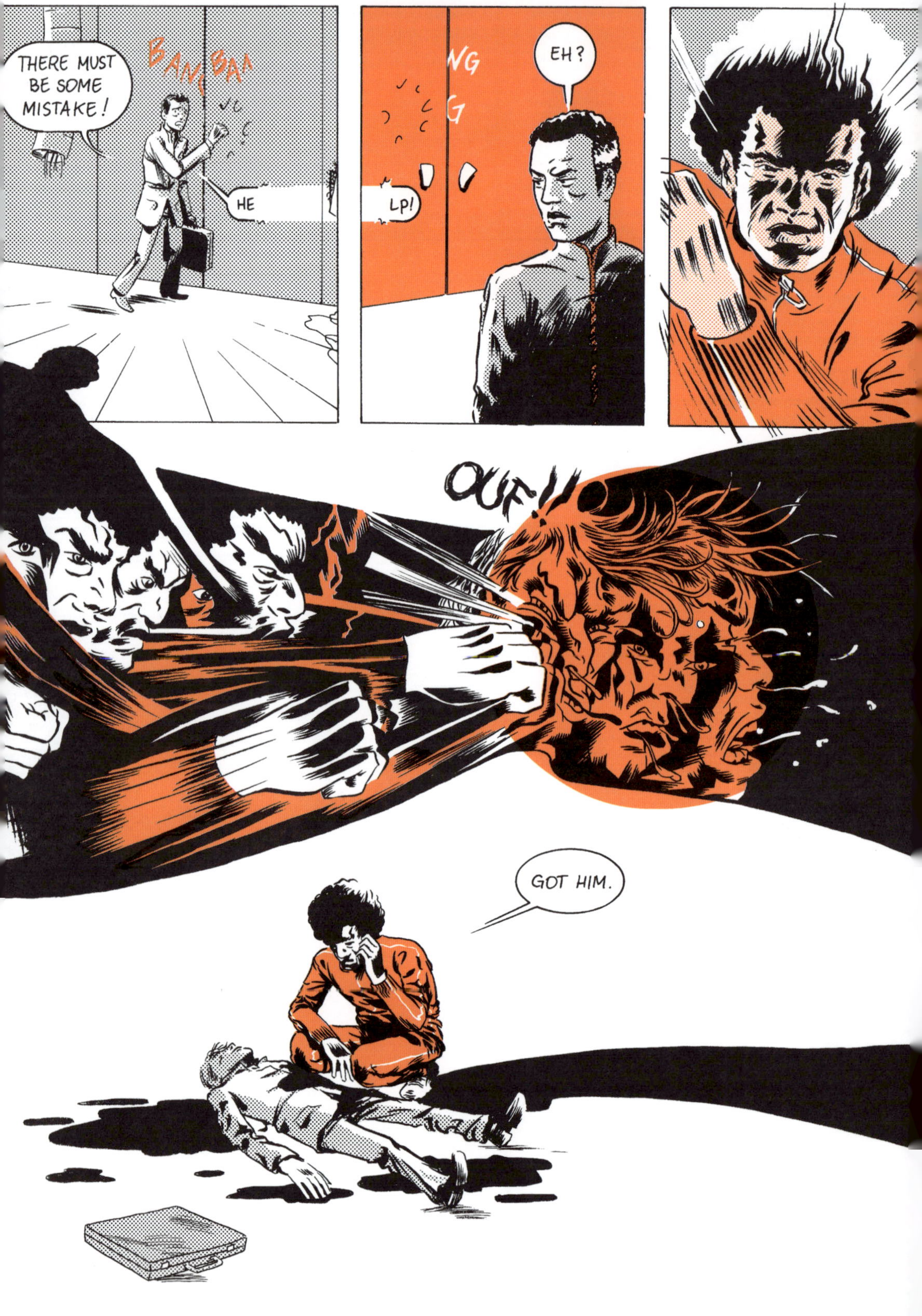
THERE MUST BE SOME MISTAKE!
BANG BAA
HE
NG
G
LP!
EH?
OUF!!
GOT HIM.

YOUR MAJESTY?
WHAT HAPPENED TO THE GUARDS?
LOCKED!
SIR!?
BRING THE CHOPPER ARO
OW...
WHAT'S GOING ON!? WHERE DID THE GUARDS GO!? WHO ARE YOU? WHAT FLOOR IS THIS!!!?
I DON'T KNOW...
THEY JUST WALKED AWAY I'M THE SECRETARY 23RD FLOOR
WHAT DO YOU WANT FROM ME...?
THROB
THE THRONE ROOM HAS BEEN COMPROMISED! I REPEAT: THE THRONE...
I APOLOGIZE FOR HAVING TO HURT YOU FURTHER.
WHA..!
THERE IS NOTHING HERE!
WHERE DID THIS ROOM COME FROM?

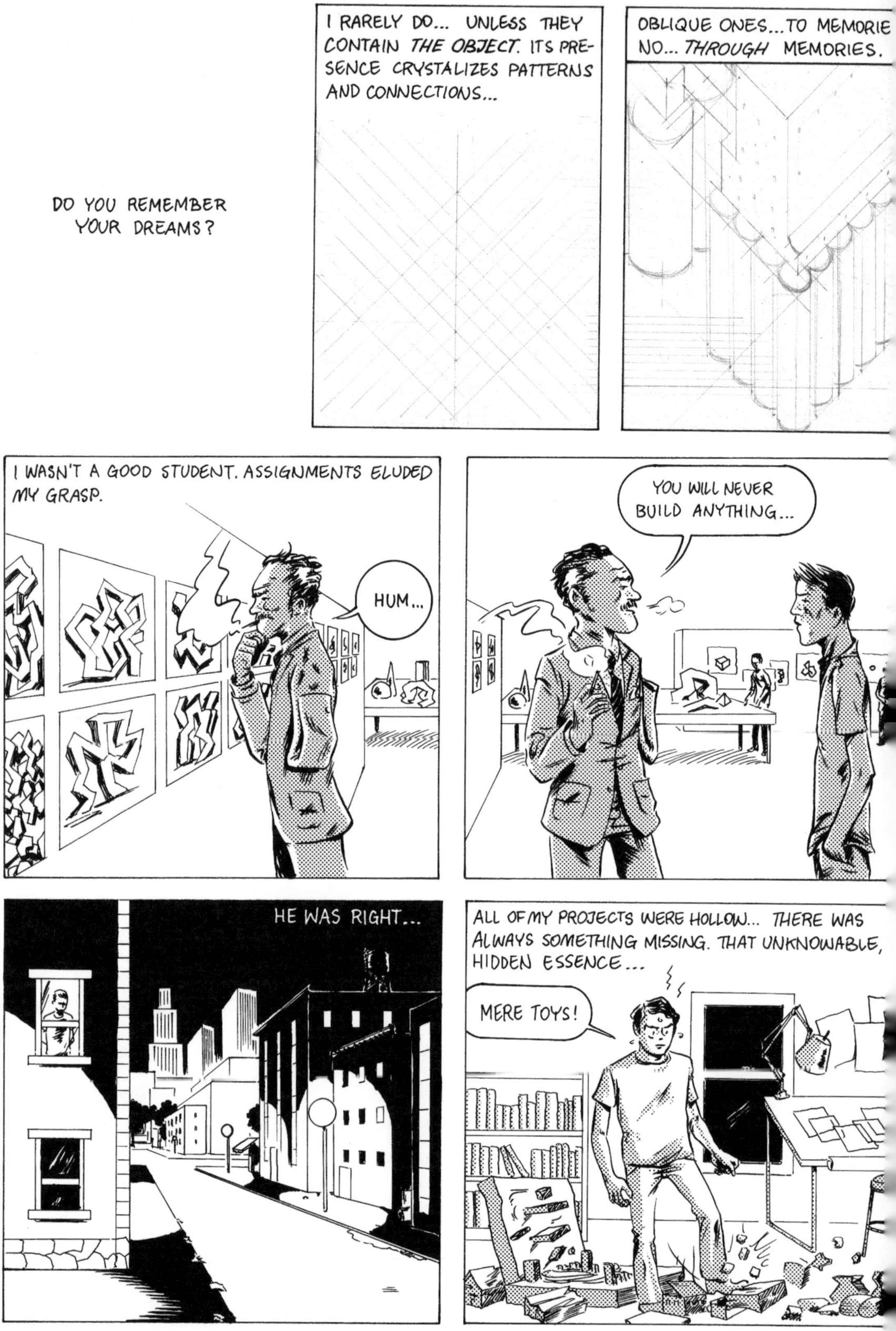
DO YOU REMEMBER YOUR DREAMS?
I RARELY DO... UNLESS THEY CONTAIN *THE OBJECT*. ITS PRESENCE CRYSTALIZES PATTERNS AND CONNECTIONS...
OBLIQUE ONES...TO MEMORIE
NO... *THROUGH* MEMORIES.
I WASN'T A GOOD STUDENT. ASSIGNMENTS ELUDED MY GRASP.
HUM...
YOU WILL NEVER BUILD ANYTHING...
HE WAS RIGHT...
ALL OF MY PROJECTS WERE HOLLOW... THERE WAS ALWAYS SOMETHING MISSING. THAT UNKNOWABLE, HIDDEN ESSENCE...
MERE TOYS!

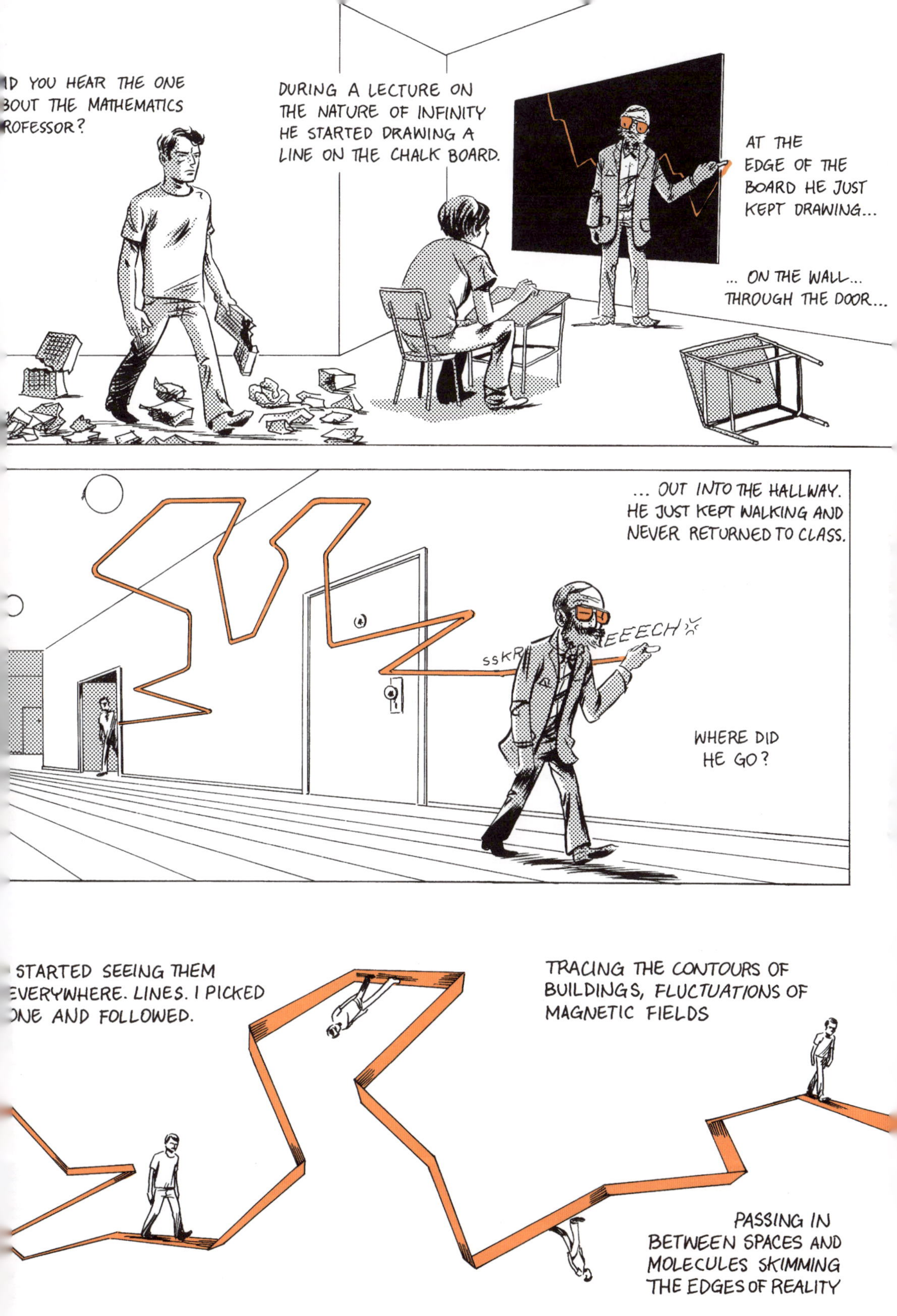
ID YOU HEAR THE ONE
BOUT THE MATHEMATICS
ROFESSOR?
DURING A LECTURE ON THE NATURE OF INFINITY HE STARTED DRAWING A LINE ON THE CHALK BOARD.
AT THE EDGE OF THE BOARD HE JUST KEPT DRAWING...
... ON THE WALL... THROUGH THE DOOR...
... OUT INTO THE HALLWAY. HE JUST KEPT WALKING AND NEVER RETURNED TO CLASS.
SSKR
EEECH
WHERE DID HE GO?
STARTED SEEING THEM
VERYWHERE. LINES. I PICKED
NE AND FOLLOWED.
TRACING THE CONTOURS OF BUILDINGS, FLUCTUATIONS OF MAGNETIC FIELDS
PASSING IN BETWEEN SPACES AND MOLECULES SKIMMING THE EDGES OF REALITY

LINES. OUTLINES, TRAJECTORIES, VECTORS, TRENDS

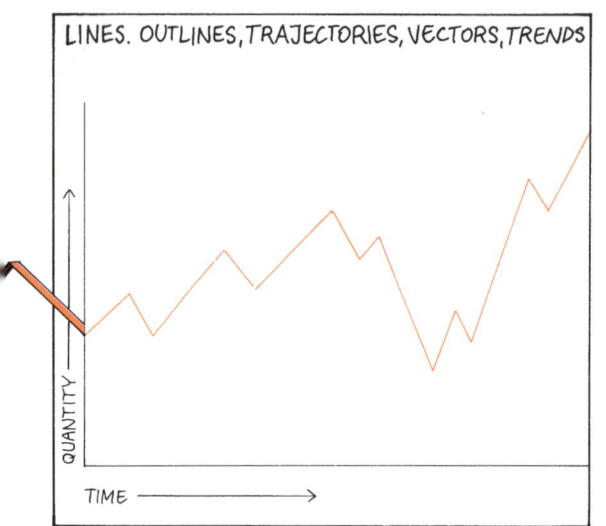

QUANTITY / TIME

DAYS LIVED IN HOTELS/YEAR
INCOME
MILES TRAVELLED
NUMBER OF PROJECTS
AMOUNT OF SLEEP/DAY

QUANTITY / TIME

GDP, POPULATIONS, MURDERS, INTEREST RATES, GRAIN FUTURES, OIL RESERVES, GAS STATIONS, VEHICLES, DENSITY, ZONING PATTERNS...

STREETS SIDEWALKS INTERSECTIONS SQUARES

BOXES ENVELOPES NEIGHBORHOODS SLUMS DISTRICTS

CITIES. URUK.

MY PROJECT!

HASI...
GOOD
YOU ARE AWAKE. THAT IS GOOD.
UH... WERE YOU WATCHING ME THE WHOLE TIME I WAS OUT?
QUIET! FOLLOW ME!
WHERE ARE
QUIET I SAID!

THE DOWNWARD MOMENTUM WAS IRRESISTABLE. EVEN WHEN I WAS CLEARLY MOVING SIDEWAYS

OR UPWARDS...

I COULDN'T SHAKE THE FEELING OF CONTINUOUS DESCENT...

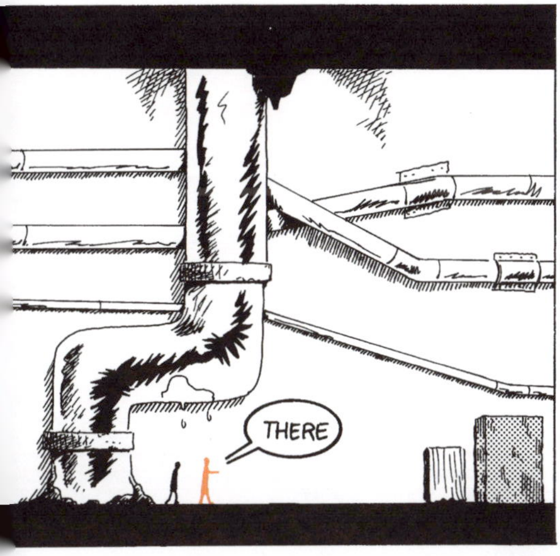
THERE

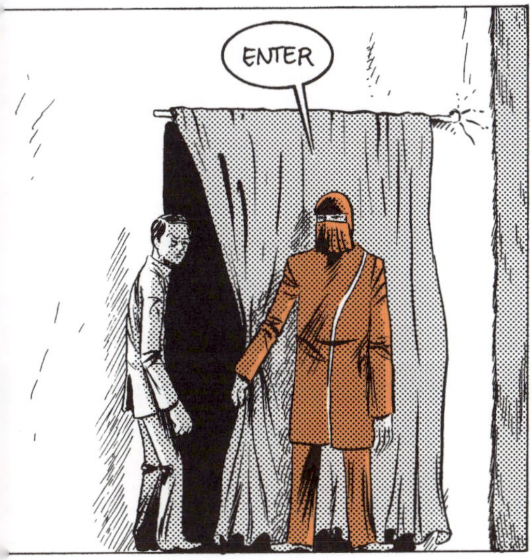
ENTER

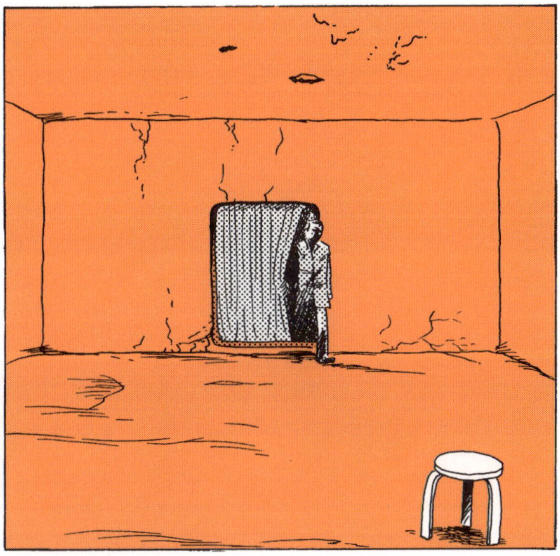

TAK TAK TAK
PLEASE MR. ______
TAK
SIT
DOWN
14 THOUSAND YEARS AGO A BOY WAS BORN. HIS NAME WAS IMHOTEP.

MHOTEP COULD SPEAK WITH STONES. HEY TAUGHT HIM TO SHAPE OCKS AND TO BUILD.
WITH THE HELP OF THE STONES HE BUILT URUK, THE FIRST CITY IN THE WORLD.
I WAS KIDNAPPED TO ENDURE A MYTHOLOGY LESSON? I KNOW THE STORY OF IMHOTEP!
NO YOU DON'T!
THIS IS THE REAL STORY!
IE STONES DIDN'T TEACH IMHOTEP BUILD URUK. THEY SHOWED HIM HERE TO EXCAVATE IT!
AN OLDER CITY WAS ALREADY HERE... AN ARTIFACT OF AN EVEN OLDER AND UNKNOWN PROTO-CIVILIZATION!
IMHOTEP WAS NOT ALLOWED TO STAY IN URUK. THE STONES TOLD HIM TO GO FORTH INTO THE WORLD AND EXCAVATE MORE CITIES.
TER MANY YEARS IMHOTEP RETURNED. DURING S ABSENCE THE PEOPLE OPENED THE TOMBS OF E ORIGINAL BUILDERS. THE CITY GREW FAT ID RICH ON EXHUMED TREASURE.
E PEOPLE EVEN WORSHIPPED STRANGE NEW DS. AND THEY BUILT FROM MUD NOT STONE!
THE STONES BECAME ANGRY AND TOLD IMHOTEP TO CAUSE A GREAT EARTHQUAKE. URUK WAS DESTROYED! MANY PEOPLE PERISHED.

THE EARTHQUAKE OPENED A GREAT CRACK AT THE CENTER OF URUK.
THE PEOPLE BEGGED IMHOTEP FOR HELP.
IMHOTEP CONSULTED THE STONES
THE STONES DEMANDED THE PEOPL
REPLENISH THE EMPTIED TOMBS.
AND THE STONES SAID: SLAUGHTER A THOUSAND SOULS YEARLY.
AND THE STONES SAID: MUMMIFY THE BODIES, AND RICHLY ADORN THEM.
AND THE STONES SAID: ENTOMB T
MUMMIES UNDER THE CITY. IMHOT
WEPT AT THIS. THIS IS NOT THE W
HE SAID.
HE TOLD THE PEOPLE TO CARVE A CHAMBER IN THE GREAT CHASM. SEAL ME INSIDE HE SAID.
BOM
BOM
AND HE SAID: BURY THE CHASM AND BUILD A GREAT PENTAGONAL PYRAMID ON TOP.
AND HE SAID: I WILL REMAIN HE
FOR ALL ETERNITY AND SOOTHE
THE STONES WITH MY TEARS.

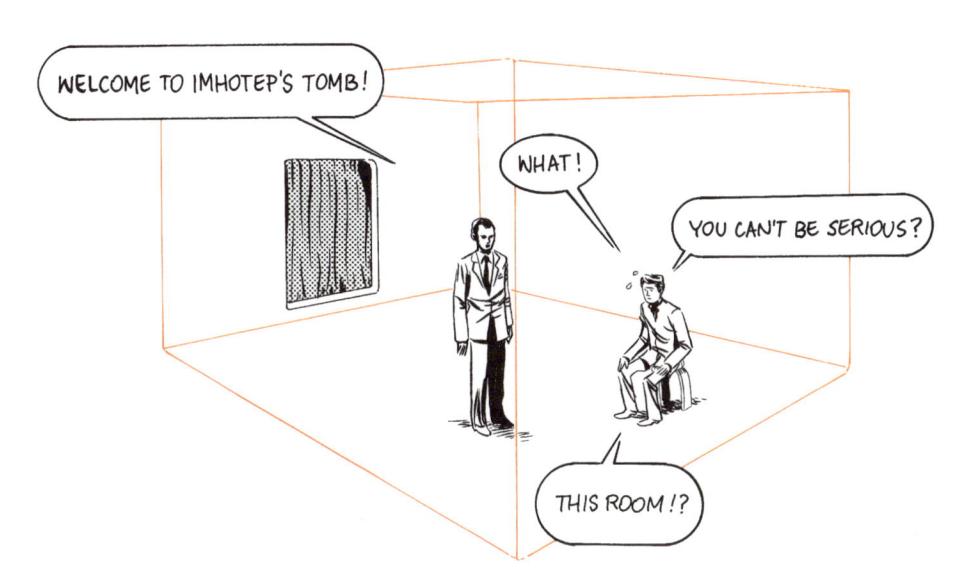

"WELCOME TO IMHOTEP'S TOMB!"

"WHAT!"

"YOU CAN'T BE SERIOUS?"

"THIS ROOM!?"

"IT HAS BEEN EMPTY FOR TOO LONG..."

"UH"

"BUT WHAT DO YOU WANT FROM ME?"

"WE DON'T WANT ANYTHING. WE ARE THE AGENTS OF THE CITY. WE LISTEN TO ITS DEMANDS."

"IT WANTS YOUR BUILDING."

"OOHKAY... I CAN WORK WITH THAT... I THINK..."

IT DOESN'T WANT TO WORK WITH YOU.
IT DIDN'T WANT IMHOTEP'S BITTER TEARS...
IT WANTS SACRIFICE.
ER...
FOR MILLENIA THE PEOPLE OF URUK ENTOMBED THOUSANDS OF SOULS TO ASSURE THE PROSPERITY OF THE CITY. PEOPLE FORGET THAT EACH ARCHAEOLOGICAL LAYER IS A CATASTROPHE. THERE ARE SO MANY LAYERS OF SUFFERING ABOVE AND BELOW... IT'S NO DIFFERENT ELSEWHERE OF COURSE... IT JUST GOES DEEPER HERE.
AND THE DEEPER YOU GO THE STRANGER IT GETS.
MILLIONS OF DEAD BECOME ONE IMHOTEP. HUMAN SHIT TURNS INTO DEPOSITS OF GOLD. THE PAST BECOMES THE FUTURE...
THE RECENT URUK RESOURCE BOOM IS LITERALL ARCHAEOLOGY. WE'RE REPEATING HISTORY, B WE'RE MORE CIVILIZED THIS TIME. WE DON'T NEE TO SACRIFICE THOUSANDS. WE HAVE MILLIONS WH COME WILLINGLY. LIFE IS BRUTAL AND SHORT IN THE SLUMS. THEY WILL SACRIFICE EVERYTHIN FOR THE ILLUSION OF A BETTER LIFE. ONCE AGA URUK RUNS ON THE DEAD.

"YOUR BUILDING HAS BEEN FINALIZED AND WILL BE APPROVED BY THE KING."

"WHAT!!"

"CONSTRUCTION WILL BEGIN SHORTLY."

"BUT THERE ARE ONLY SKETCHES! I HAVEN'T SHOWN THEM TO ANYONE!"

"SEAL IT!"

"YOUR BUILDING WILL BE MAGNIFICENT. A NEW BEGINNING."

RIPP

"IT WILL TAKE THE CRITICS BY SURPRISE. YOUR CAREER WILL BE RE-ASSESSED."

WHRAK

"THE CITY NEEDS A NEW IMHOTEP."

WHRRK

HOW LONG HAVE I BEEN SITTING IN THE DARK?

I THOUGHT I'D HAVE SUFFOCATED BY NOW...

I MUST BE HALLUCINATING.

DID I READ SOMEWHERE THAT SOME ANCIENT TOMBS WERE PAINTED WITH RADIOACTIVE PIGMENT?

THOK

SHHH...

WAS THAT A SOUND?

THOK

THOK THOK

THOK THOK
THOK THOK

THOK

CRUMBL

OW!
?
GOLD?
GOLD HERE!?
WAS HE IMHOTEP?
NO. THERE IS NOTHING HERE.
GRUNT
I LEFT THROUGH THE OPENING.
WEIRDLY, THE TUNNEL LED DOWNWARDS.
IT WAS LIT BY A STRANGE BIOLUMINESCENCE.

SPACE

- 100,000 MILES

- 10,000 Miles

C 30
M 40
Y 0
K 0

SKYWAY SLEEPLES

First appearance: *Twin Cities Noir*, 2013

- 1,000 Miles

- 100 Miles

- 1 Mile

1,000,000,000 BC   1,000,000 BC   500,000 BC   40,000

TIME

2000 AD   10,000 AD

WHY DO I LIVE IN THE SKYWAYS?
LET ME ANSWER WITH A QUESTION.
HAVE YOU EVER WANTED TO LIVE
IN THE FUTURE?

SKYWAY SLEEPLESS

THE AVERAGE COMMUTER IS BLIND TO THE POTENTIAL OF THE SKYWAYS... THEY CAN AVOID THE WEATHER OR TRAFFIC... BUT...

DO THEY FEEL THE WEIGHTLESSNESS?...
WALKING THE SKYWAYS IS LIKE FLOATING THROUGH A CITY-SIZED SPACE STATION...

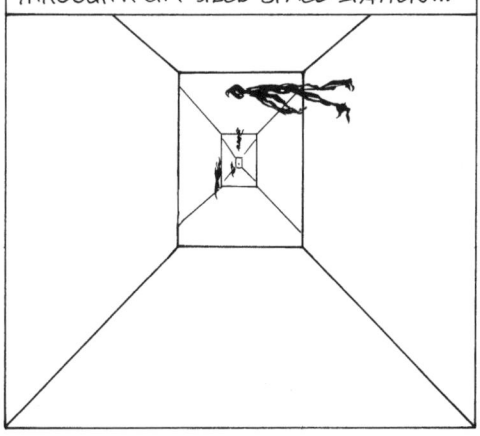

TOMORROW THE SKYWAYS WILL BECOME... **SKYLAB**: FESTIVAL OF EXPERIENTIAL ART.
THAT LOOKS GOOD, DEAR.
PROFESSOR ECKE!?
AH! MY BEST PUPIL! A SHAME YOU NEVER BECAME AN ARCHITECT!
AH...
NEVER MIND! LET ME TELL YOU ABOUT MY NEXT PROJECT... ENDLESS SKYWAY.
HEY PROF, I'M GONNA GET SOME COFFEE...
OH GOOD! PLEASE BRING ME A DOUBLE ESPRESSO! DANKE, ANITA!
SURE THING!
LATE NIGHT, PROF?
I'M AN OLD MAN...
I DON'T NEED MUCH SLEEP... BUT I MUST BE ALERT... NOW LET ME EXPLAIN...
WE MAY HAVE THE LARGEST SKYWAY SYSTEM IN THE WORLD... BUT IT ISN'T ENOUGH! YOU SEE, CITIES ARE THE BRAINS OF HUMANITY... THE STREETS FORM THE BASIC CONNECTIONS FOR THE LIFE OF THE CITY... BUT SKYWAYS, THEY ARE THE HIGHER FUNCTIONS... ON THE SKYWAY LEVEL WE CAN APPREHEND THE WORLD BELOW... WE CAN GRASP IT IN ONE VISTA! THE CONTINUOUS EVOLUTION OF THE HUMAN RACE MUST BE ACCOMPANIED BY THE EVOLUTION OF THE CITY! ENDLESS SKYWAY IS A SYSTEM OF CONNECTIONS TO ALLOW THE CITY TO KEEP PACE... IT MUST START WITH A **NEW** SKYWAY LEVEL!... WITH **DIAGONAL** SKYWAYS! THE FIRST STEP TO AN ENDLESS **EVOLUTION**...
UH... SORRY, PROF... I GOTTA GO NOW...
ECKE'S WORDS ECHOED IN MY SKULL FOR SOME TIME...
WHAT'S THIS?

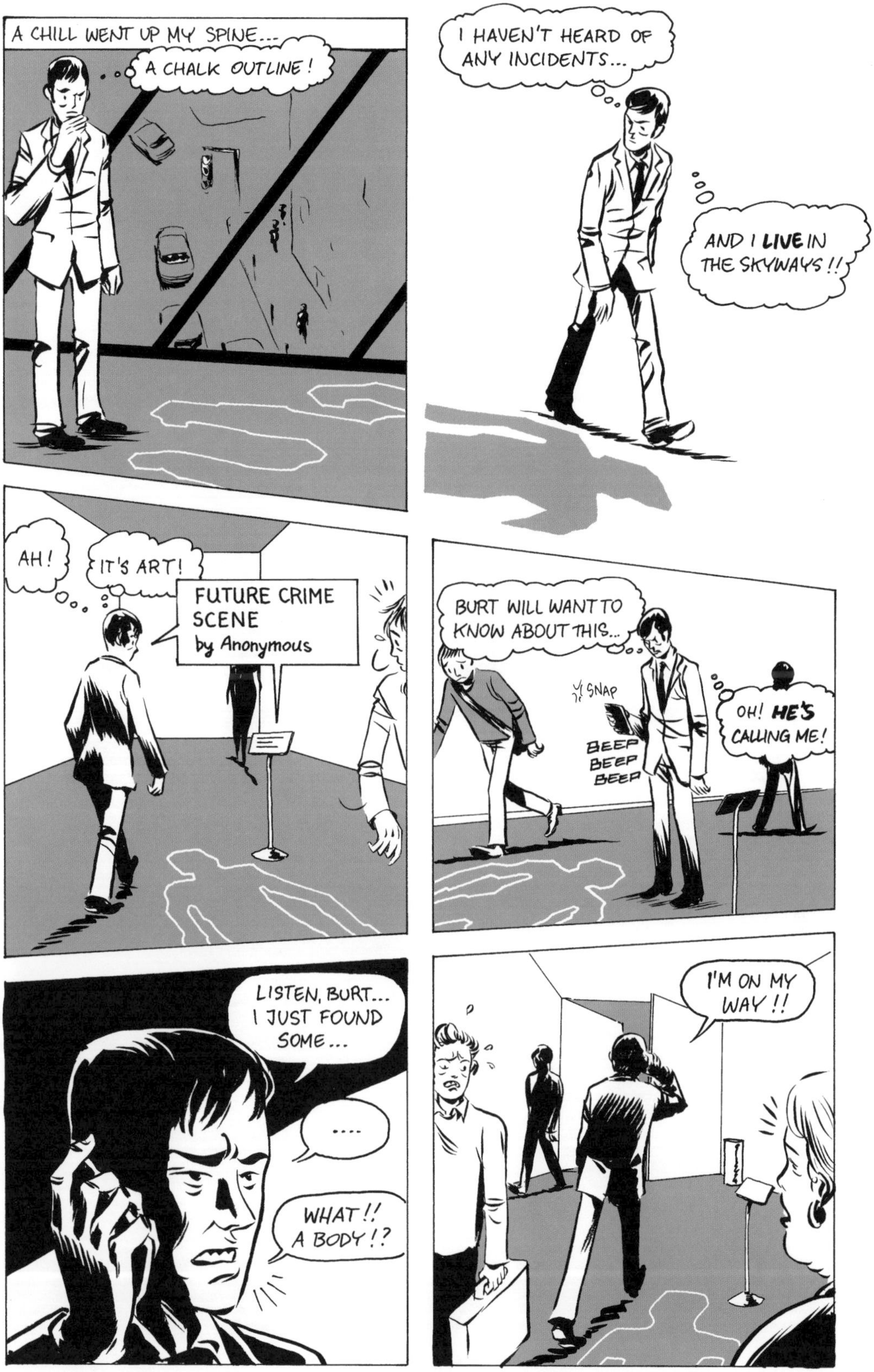
A CHILL WENT UP MY SPINE...
A CHALK OUTLINE!
I HAVEN'T HEARD OF ANY INCIDENTS...
AND I LIVE IN THE SKYWAYS!!
AH!
IT'S ART!
FUTURE CRIME SCENE by Anonymous
BURT WILL WANT TO KNOW ABOUT THIS...
SNAP
BEEP BEEP BEEP
OH! HE'S CALLING ME!
LISTEN, BURT... I JUST FOUND SOME...
....
WHAT!! A BODY!?
I'M ON MY WAY!!

MORE OF THEM !?
FUTURE CRIME WAVE
by Anonymous
STOP SHOVING!
LET ME SEE
WHAT'S GOING ON ?
HUH !?
LET ME THROUGH! SKYWAY SECURITY!
OH GOOD ! YOU'RE HERE.
HEY!
GET IN LINE!
WHO ?
CAN YOU BELIEVE THIS !? EVERYONE IS FREAKED...
WHA !!
ANITA ?
YOU KNOW HER ?!
I THINK SHE'S PROF ECKE'S INTERN OR SOMETHING...
WE GOTTA GET HER OUTTA HERE!
CAN'T SEE...
MURDER...
C'MON PEOPLE! DISPERSE!
THIS COULD SPARK A PANIC!
BTW, WHY DO YOU STILL HAVE YOUR BADGE... ?
WHY DO YOU KEEP CALLING ME ?
FAIR ENOUGH!
UHHHH

WHAT HAPPENED?
HUH !!?
SHE'S NOT DEAD!?
I DIDN'T SAY SHE WAS! SHE WAS ASLEEP!
I THINK I NEED SOME COFFEE...
I FEEL
PRETTY SILLY...
THE CREEPY ART PROJECT AND ANITA'S NARCOLEPTIC FIT RATTLED THE SKYWAY RESIDENTS...
LOUNGE
HEHE! YOU SHOULD'VE SEEN YOUR FACE WHEN YOU SAW ME WAKE UP!
LAUGH IT UP! YOU LOOKED DEAD!
HEH
SO
YOU WORK HERE?
NAH... BUT I GET TO MAKE MY OWN DRINKS.
ANYWAY, WHAT HAPPENED!?
DUNNO... TOO MUCH WORK FOR THE PROF... MAYBE?
THE SKYWAYS ALWAYS PUT ME IN A TRANCE...
... A GOOD PLACE TO PLAN WORLD DOMINATION...
WORLD DOMINATION!?
YOU KNOW... PROJECTS... ECKE HAS ALL KINDS OF AMBITIOUS IDEAS...

IDEAS. PLANS. PROJECTS. I HEARD THEM ALL. ECKE'S ENDLESS SKYWAY PROJECT WITH ITS DIAGONAL SKY BRIDGES WAS INSPIRED BY BARON HAUSSMANN'S PARIS...

...LIKE THE BARON'S BOULEVARDS, AESTHETICS WERE SUBSERVIENT TO SECURITY... BUT THE SKYWAYS COULD BE SO MUCH MORE... REMOVED FROM THE DIN OF THE STREET... ER... ELEVATED... A PERFECT PLACE FOR A NEW SOCIETY...

CRAP! IT'S CLOSED... LET'S GO BACK...

A CITY OF THE SUN... IN THE SKY... RECLAIMING THE FUTURE THE SKYWAY'S WERE DESIGNED TO BRING ABOUT...

WE'RE TRAPPED!

SHHH

MY HEAD WAS SPINNING...

I AGREED WITH EVERY WORD... AND MORE...

WE WERE TRAPPED ON THE SKYWAY, SUSPENDED BETWEEN BUILDINGS... BETWEEN FUTURES... IN SOME KIND OF INDETERMINATE STATE FULL OF POSSIBILITIES...

WEIGHTLESS...

WAKE UP!
YOU OK, PAL? WHAT THE HELL IS GOING ON?
ANITA ...? WHERE...?
I, UH...GOT TRAPPED... DID YOU, UH... SEE ANITA ANYWHERE?
THAT CHICK FROM YESTERDAY? NO. LISTEN...
YOU'RE NOT THE ONLY SLEEPER... THERE ARE MORE... I GOTTA GO TAKE CARE OF...
I THINK ECKE MIGHT BE INVOLVED...
THE ARCHITECT?
YEAH... CALL IN SOME BACK UP!
UH, OK.
GOOD ...
I NEED TO FIND ANITA...
FIND HER HOW? I'VE NO IDEA WHERE TO START...
UH
DID I TAKE A WRONG ...
TURN?

PROFESSOR ECKE...
WHAT'S HE UP TO?
MORE SKYWAY SECURITY? HE'LL GET IT...
BUT WH
HOW DOES HE PULL IT OFF? HOW DOES HE PUT PEOPLE TO SLEEP?
IS THE SKYWAY SYSTEM A MACHINE TO CONTROL THE CITY? A SLEEPING GAS DELIVERY SYSTEM...?
HAS HE BEEN PLANNING THIS FOR DECADES?
A SKYWAY REPUBLIC WITH ECKE AS ARCHITECT-KING?

WAKE UP!

MAYBE YOU CAN TELL ME ...
?

WHAT THE HELL IS GOING ON ?!
ARE THEY...
ALIVE? YES... SLEEPING...
....
LOOKS LIKE ...
FREEZE !!!
...THE FEDS ARE HERE.
QUIET!

IT WAS ALL A PERFORMANCE OF COURSE... THE FEDS BRIEFLY PURSUED A PSYCHOLOGICAL TERROR CHARGE, BUT IT WENT NOWHERE...

THERE WAS ONE DEATH (RULED ACCIDENTAL). PROF ECKE STUMBLED ONTO THE HAPPENING AND... HIS HEART GAVE OUT... THOUGH AUTOPSY RESULTS WERE INCONCLUSIVE... ANITA TOOK IT HARD...

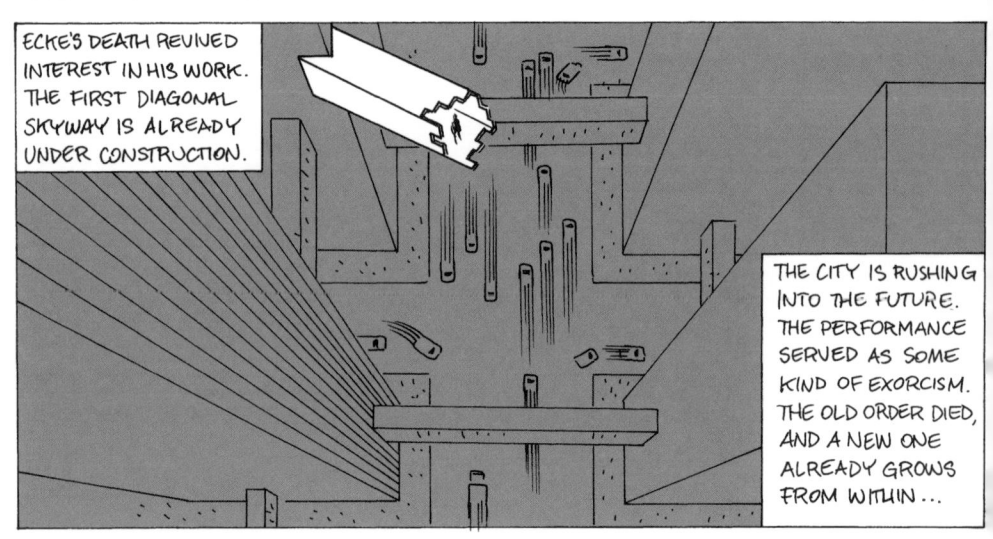

AS DID I.

BUT IT GOT A LOT OF PRESS! SKYLAB SAW A BIG SURGE IN ATTENDANCE... IT IS NOW CONSIDERED ONE THE MOST ADVANCED ART FESTIVALS...

ECKE'S DEATH REVIVED INTEREST IN HIS WORK. THE FIRST DIAGONAL SKYWAY IS ALREADY UNDER CONSTRUCTION.

THE CITY IS RUSHING INTO THE FUTURE. THE PERFORMANCE SERVED AS SOME KIND OF EXORCISM. THE OLD ORDER DIED, AND A NEW ONE ALREADY GROWS FROM WITHIN...

END

SPACE

- 100,000 MILES

- 10,000 Miles

C 0
M 80
Y 80
K 0

36TH CHAMBER OF COMMERCE

First appearance: *World War 3 Illustrated 49*, 2018

- 1,000 Miles

- 100 Miles

- 1 Mile

1,000,000,000 BC   1,000,000 BC   500,000 BC   40,00

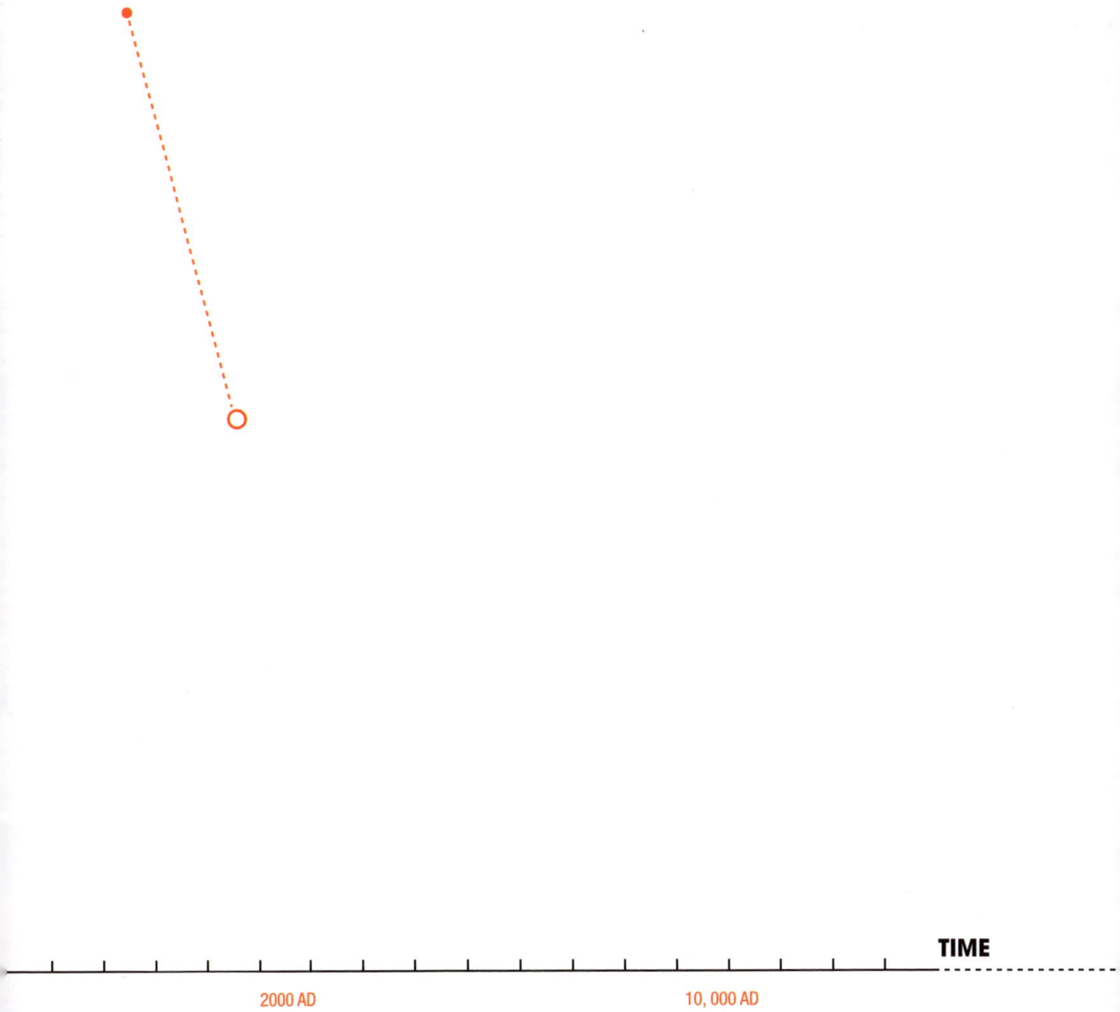
TIME
2000 AD
10, 000 AD

PROPER JOBS. WE HATE THEM, BUT IT'S THE SYSTEM.
WE GO ALONG WITH IT. THERE ISN'T MUCH CHOICE.
SEX SELLS!
BOSS
WE'RE NEVER FREE.
Shop!
PARTICIPATION IS MANDATORY AND STRICTLY CONTROLLED.
NEW!
OUR VAGUE NEEDS SATISFIED BY THE SYSTEM
OUR DREAMS CIRCUMSCRIBED

FREELANCERS OF THE WORLD, SET YOUR ROUTINE ON STUN!

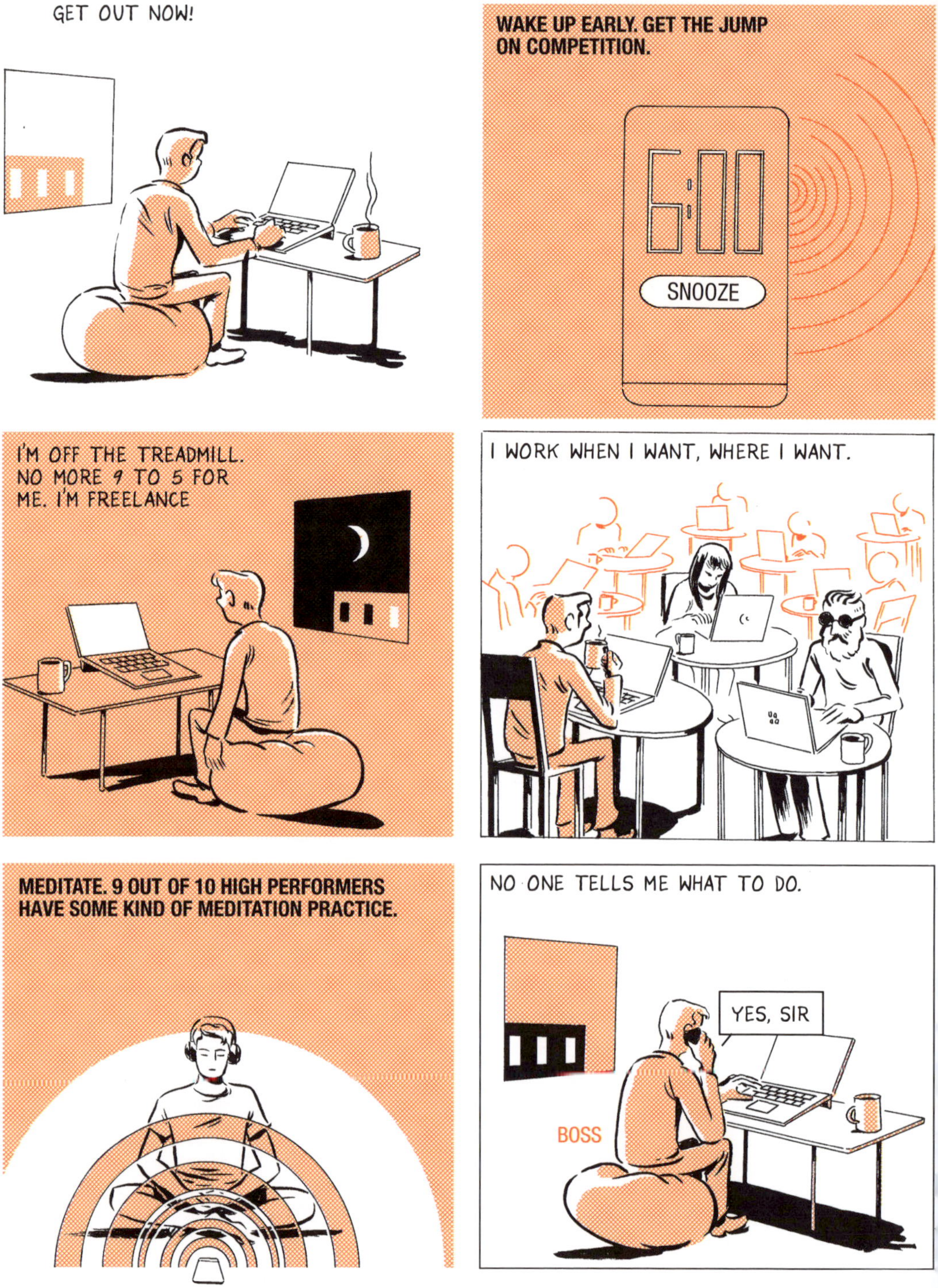

BILLS HAVE TO BE PAID

GRATITUDE. BEING GRATEFUL IMPROVES YOUR MOOD. BETTER MOOD, BETTER PERFORMANCE.

1. I'm grateful this project is done ... I think?
2. ...

EXCEPT MY CLIENTS... BUT I GET TO CHOOSE MY CLIENTS

SURE I CAN DO THAT.

MOST OF THE TIME.

TONIGHT?

WORK OUT. EXERCISE INCREASES BLOOD FLOW TO THE BRAIN. IT WILL BOOST YOUR PERFORMANCE.

BUT I'VE GOT CONTROL

I CAN CHARGE MORE!
SKIP BREAKFAST. BULLETPROOF COFFEE WILL SUPERCHARGE YOUR MORNING.
WHERE ARE THOSE FILES?
ALMOST DONE
WE NEED THEM NOW. IT'S PAST DUE!
...
SELECT FILE:
PROJECT_ZETA.PSD
UPLOAD
COLD SHOWER. IMPROVES YOUR IMMUNE SYSTEM. LOSE LESS WORK DAYS.
TOMORROW I'M SEEING A MOVIE.

36TH CHAMBER OF SHAOLIN IS MORE THAN A MOVIE.
LIU—A NOBODY—THROUGH TRAINING AND AMBITION MASTERS ALL 35 DISCIPLINES OF SHAOLIN KUNG-FU.
LIKE A KUNG-FU ELON MUSK, HE INNOVATES NEW STYLES AND FOUNDS...
THE 36TH CHAMBER
A GAME CHANGER... HE SHARES HIS MASTERY WITH OTHERS
TO HELP THEM DEFEND AGAINST THE EVIL GOVERNMENT.

RITUAL, ROUTINE, AND DISCIPLINE. THE BODY IS A TEMPLE.

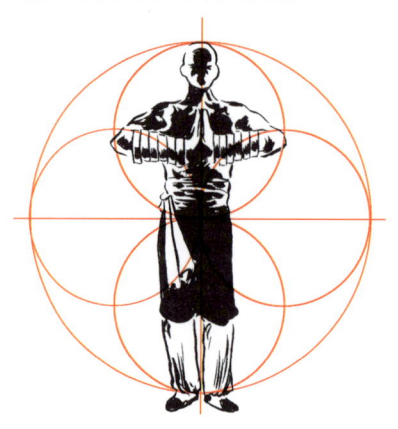

LIU BECOMES A ONE-MAN-TEMPLE OF SHAOLIN.

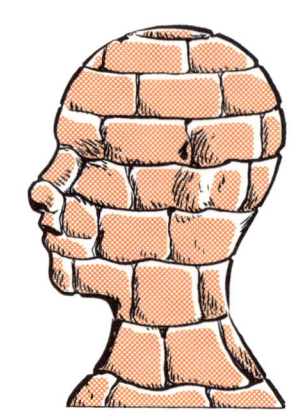

RITUAL, ROUTINE, AND DISCIPLINE. THE MODERN BODY IS A CORPORATION.

BUT WE DON'T HAVE TO FIGHT THE EVIL EMPIRE ANYMORE.

THE CHAMBERS ARE DIFFERENT TODAY.

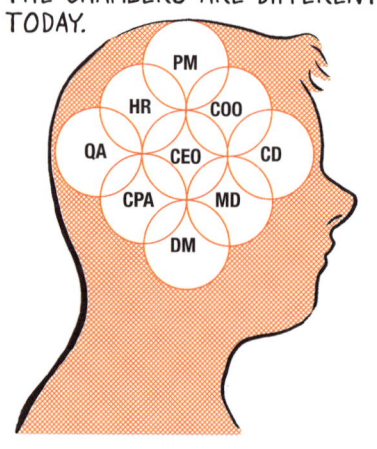

PM, HR, COO, QA, CEO, CD, CPA, MD, DM

ONE-MAN CORPORATION: MARKET ORIENTED, FLEXIBLE, FAST, INVINCIBLE.

POINTER BOSS STIM

MOBILE

IDEATION CLOUD

SUCH A GOOD MOVIE!
THE END
BZZZZT
DID YOU GET MY FILES? EVERYTHING OK?
I'M SORRY BUT THE COMPANY IS LIQUIDATING...
THE END
WE WILL NOT BE USING YOUR WORK.
BUT YOU OWE ME $15,000...
WE WILL PAY $2,000 IN CASH AND THE REST IN FURNITURE. WE HAVE AERON CHAIRS...
I DON'T NEED AN AERON CHAIR...
WE CAN OFFER THEM AT HALF PRICE...
THERE'S ALSO EAMES LOUNGE AND OTTOMAN...
HELLO?

LABOR=MONEY=OBJECT=MONEY=LABOR
EXCHANGE VALUE GOES BOTH WAYS.
BARTER WAS SUPPOSED TO HAVE BEEN SUPPLANTED, BUT THE SYSTEM IS FLUID.
I HAVE TO BE MORE FLEXIBLE... STRONGER
OH!
I CAN TURN THE FURNITURE BACK INTO CASH.
OFFICE FURNITURE [FOR SALE]
SPONSORED
HELLO...
REVOLUTIONARY KUNG-FU
SPONSORED
... WHAT'S THIS?
REVOLUTIONARY KUNG-FU
BREAK THE BOX!
IN LIFE & BUSINESS
SIGN UP NOW
MY NEW ROUTINE... ?

SPACE

— 100,000 MILES

— 10,000 Miles

PMS 3245
UTOPIA DIVIDEND
Previously unpublished.

— 1,000 Miles

— 100 Miles

— 1 Mile

1,000,000,000 BC　　　1,000,000 BC　　　500,000 BC　　　40,000

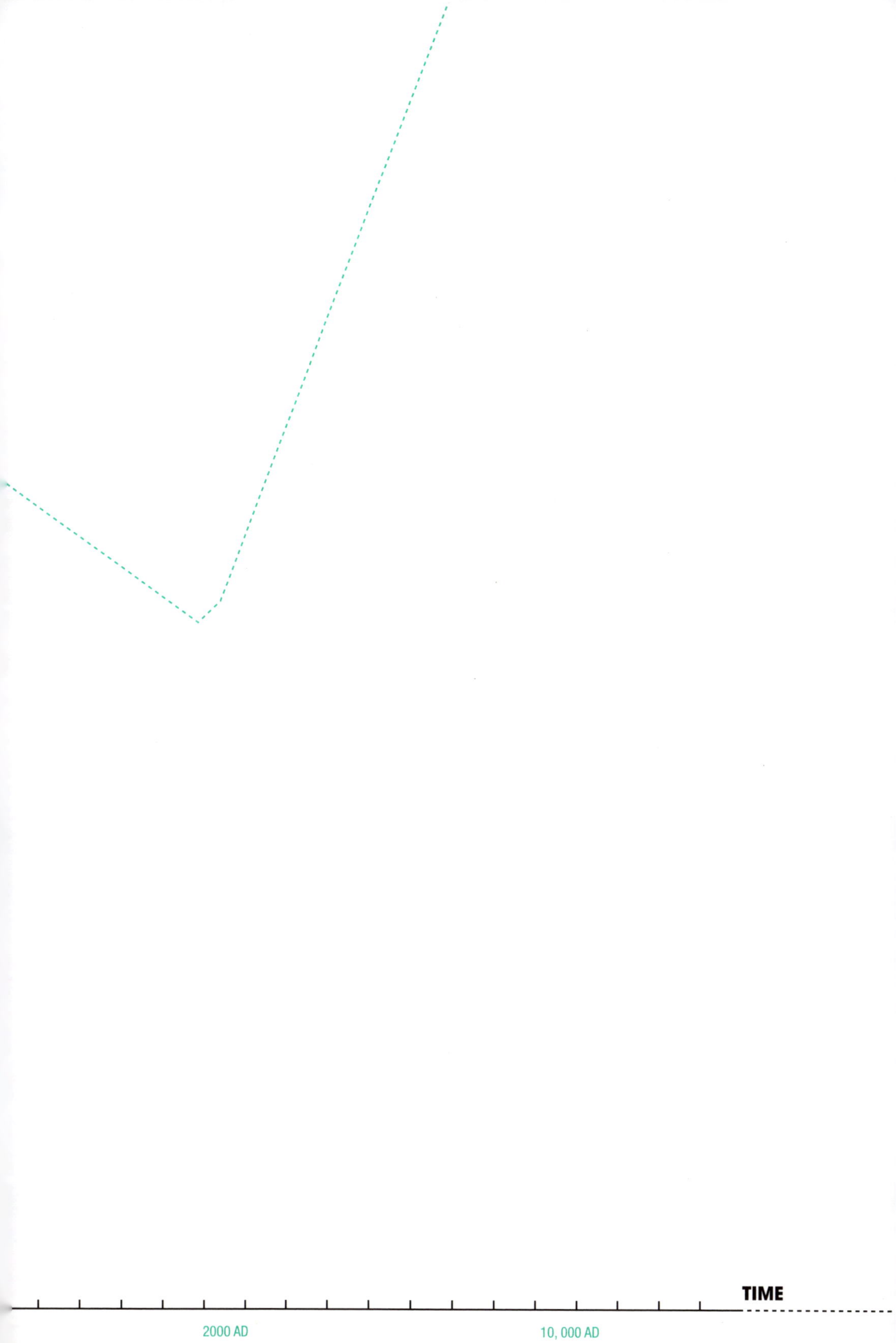

2000 AD   10, 000 AD   **TIME**

THE OCEAN STRETCHED ENDLESSLY BELOW...

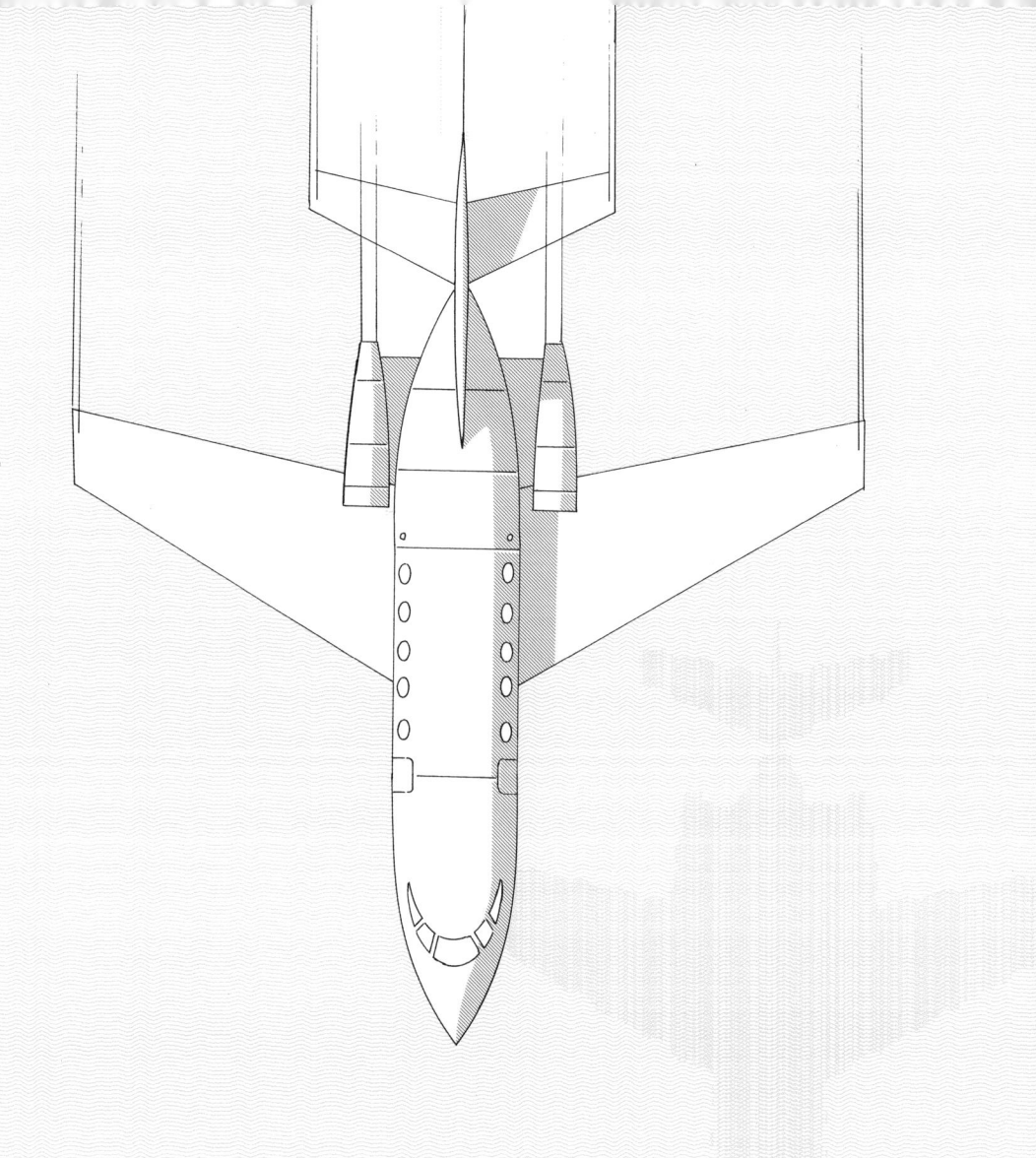

WATER COVERS SEVENTY PERCENT OF THE PLANET. IN DEEP CLIMATE CYCLES, LAND HAS EMERGED AND SUBMERGED COUNTLESS TIMES. WHAT ENTITIES AWAIT IN ATLANTEAN DEPTHS BELOW, READY TO SURFACE...

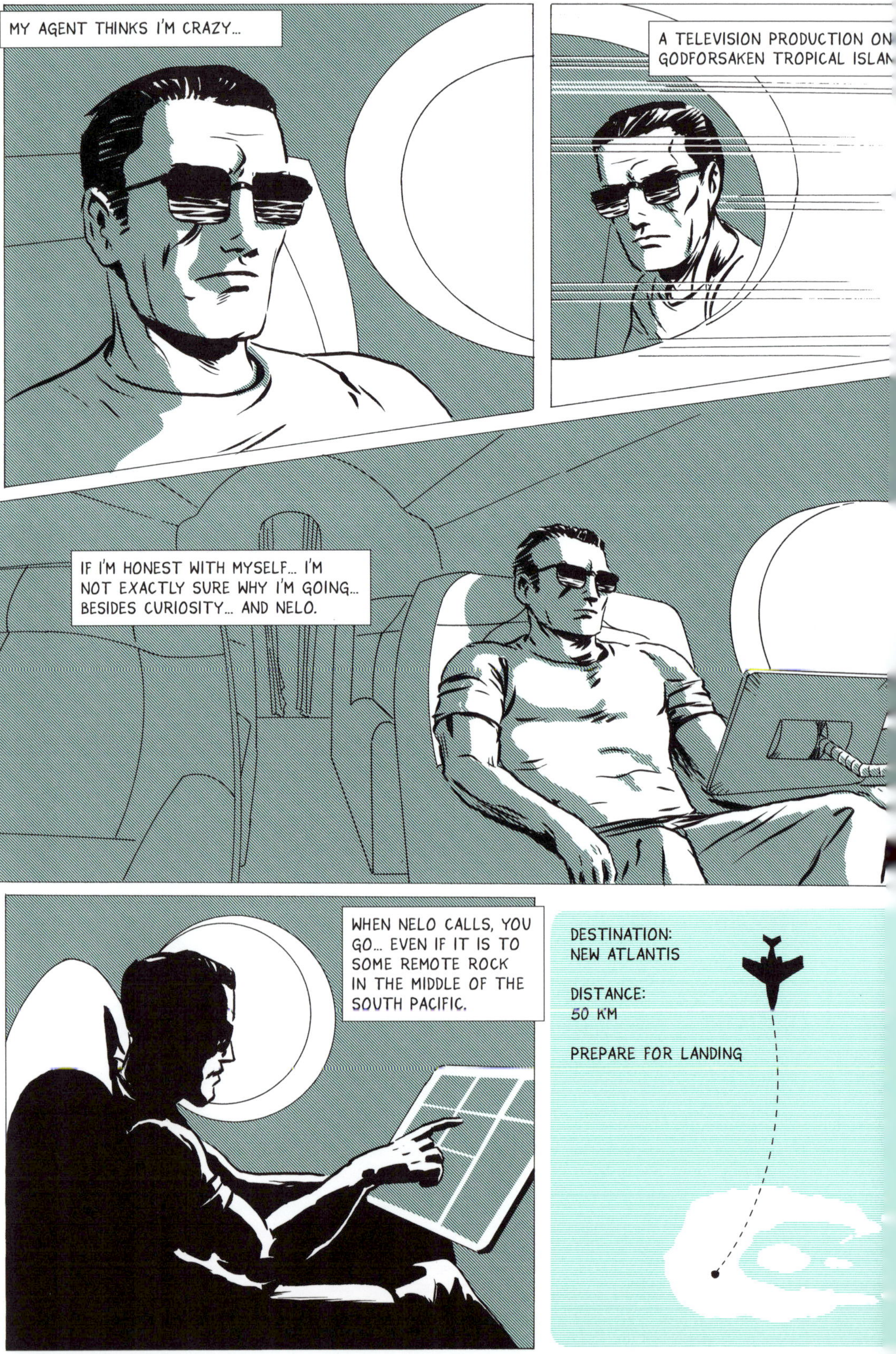
MY AGENT THINKS I'M CRAZY...
A TELEVISION PRODUCTION ON GODFORSAKEN TROPICAL ISLAN
IF I'M HONEST WITH MYSELF... I'M NOT EXACTLY SURE WHY I'M GOING... BESIDES CURIOSITY... AND NELO.
WHEN NELO CALLS, YOU GO... EVEN IF IT IS TO SOME REMOTE ROCK IN THE MIDDLE OF THE SOUTH PACIFIC.
DESTINATION: NEW ATLANTIS
DISTANCE: 50 KM
PREPARE FOR LANDING

WELCOME TO LEMURIA!
I THOUGHT THIS WAS ____?
"WAS" IS THE OPERATIVE WORD.
THINGS TEND TO CHANGE QUICKLY HERE. THINGS THAT WERE NO LONGER ARE...
THIS IS LEMURIA.
I'M CONFUSED...
NO NEED
FOLLOW ME, IT'LL CLEAR UP QUICKLY
ALMOST THERE
WELCOME TO LEMURIA, AND THE SET OF NEW ATLANTIS.
IT LOOKED UNREAL... THE SET WAS MASSIVE. LIKE A SMALL CITY... WITH ITS OWN SPACE AND CONTAINER PORTS... AND A ZIGGURAT?

IT ALL STARTED AS A SPACE-FAN LIVE STREAM. HE WANTED TO TRACK THE PROGRESS ON NELO'S REVOLUTIONARY ROCKET.

WHO KNEW DISRUPTING THE SPACE INDUSTRY WOULD CAPTURE RATINGS GOLD IN A WORLD DROWNING IN TIRED VIRTUAL MIASMA OF REBOOTS, SEQUELS, REVIVALS...

A LOOSE NETWORK OF YOUTUBE ENTHUSIASTS, PIRATE RADIOS, AND HAM RADIO OPERATORS GENERATED A HUGE AUDIENCE.

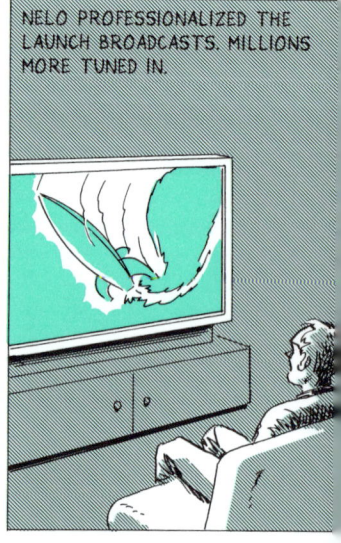

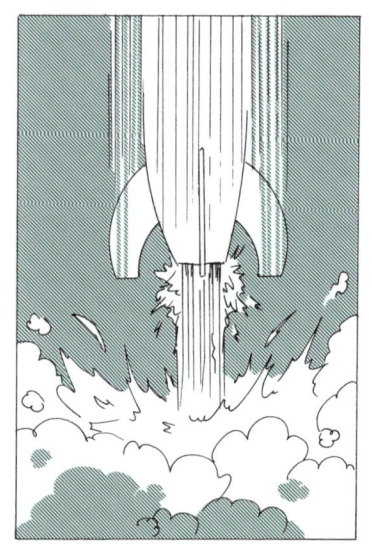

NELO SEIZED THE OPPORTUNITY

HIS SPACE PROGRAMMING BECAME EXCLUSIVE ON AETHERNET, HIS GLOBAL SATELLITE NETWORK

VIEWERS FLOCKED TO SPACE TV, AND AETHERNET BECAME A BIG PLAYER IN THE GLOBAL MEDIA ECOSYSTEM.

NELO PROFESSIONALIZED THE LAUNCH BROADCASTS. MILLIONS MORE TUNED IN.

MALCOLM --- WAS HIRED AS DIRECTOR OF PROGRAMMING. HE CONVINCED NELO TO ACQUIRE THIS ISLAND AS A PLATFORM...

... TO LAUNCH NEW... ORGINAL PROGRAMMING.

NEW ATLANTIS. MALCOLM JOKED THAT IT WAS AN ADAPTATION OF FRANCIS BACON'S TRACT...

NOT JUST A NEW "GAME OF THRONES" FOR NELO FANS.

ALCOLM'S APPROACH WAS STRICT METHOD... ALL CTORS AND CREW HAD TO LIVE IN NEW ATLANTIS AS IT WAS A REAL PLACE... I DIDN'T HAVE MUCH TO DO... ESIDES A COMPLETE COMMUNICATION BLACK-OUT

DEEP MEDITATION

SUN AND STEEL

NCIENT WEAPONS TRAINING

HAND-TO-HAND COMBAT

NOTHING I HADN'T DONE BEFORE... BUT HERE, AWAY FROM THE WORLD, THE VIBE WAS DIFFERENT...

WAS IT A COINCIDENCE THAT THE ISLAND WAS ALSO A SOURCE OF A RARE VOLCANIC INGREDIENT? THE KEY TO A NEW SUPER-STRONG CONCRETE — STRONGER THAN ROMAN CONCRETE — THAT COULD BE USED ON ROCKET PADS OR MARS.	MINERS STUMBLED ON PREVIOUSLY UNDISCOVERED ROCK ART DATING BACK TO THE ICE AGE... THIS UPENDED THE ACCEPTED HISTORY OF THE REGION.
THE DISCOVERY LIFTED TO PROMINENCE HEHU, A LOCAL ARTISAN WHO WAS NOW UNDERSTOOD TO BE WORKING IN AN INCREDIBLY ANCIENT ARTISTIC TRADITION...	RUMORED TO BE 200+ YEARS-OLD... LEGEND SAYS THAT AS A BOY, HEHU SAW MYSTERIOUS MEGASTRUCTURES BRIEFLY REVEALED BY THE KRAKATOA TSUNAMI.
THEN HEHU DECLARED NELO TO BE SENT BY THE GODS... IT BECAME A BIT OF A SCANDAL... NELO WAS ACCUSED OF TAKING ADVANTAGE. INSTEAD OF RUNNING FROM IT, NELO ADOPTED HEHU'S ANCIENT ICONOGRAPHY INTO HIS BRANDING.	THE NEW ATLANTIS SET BECAME THE TESTING GROUND FOR THE NEW CONCRETE... AFTER STRESS TESTS WERE COMPLETED, IT BECAME CLEAR THAT THE CENTRAL ZIGGURAT SET PIECE WOULD OUTLIVE THE PYRAMIDS OF GIZA.

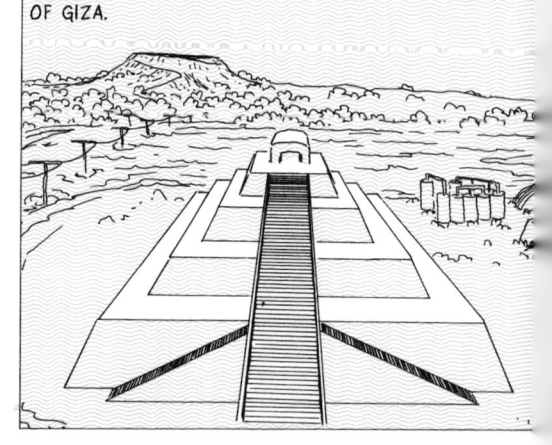

E STILL HAD CAST PARTIES... NELO'S PRESENCE TTRACTED AN ODD ENTOURAGE... HIS GIRLFRIEND, RIMES, WAS A FREQUENT VISITOR.
YOU'RE NOT AS BIG AS I IMAGINED
SO I SAID, "FUCK IT, LET'S BUILD A ZIGURRAT!"
THERE WAS WEIRD ENERGY IN THE AIR... A STRANGE ALIGNMENT OF ANCIENT AND NEW... THE SET TOOK ON A NEW SIGNIFICANCE AND OUTSIZED REALITY.
R HOST NATION, ---, ON THE OTHER HAND BEGAN) RESEMBLE A THEATRICAL SET... THE PARLIAMENT A IEMEPARK MINIATURE VERSION OF THE REAL THING. IEIR ECONOMY BECAME DOMINATED BY NELO IN NO TIME.
ITS CULTURE, A CURIOUS MELANGE OF FOREIGN INFLUENCES, BETRAYED A LONG HISTORY OF COLONIZATION.
WELCOME, NELO
WHAT'S UP?
NELO'S INDUSTRIAL EMPIRE WAS AN IRRESISTABLE FORCE
MORE REAL THAN ANY NATION
ANSPORT
NETWORK
SPACE
TUNNELS

DAY-TO-DAY IT DIDN'T SEEM LIKE WE WERE FILMING ANYTHING. OCCASIONALLY A SMALL CREW SHOWED UP TO FILM A TRAINING SESSION OR SOMETHING... I DIDN'T REALLY KNOW WHAT MY ROLE WAS.

MALCOLM SEEMED SATISFIED SO I PUT IT OUT OF MY MIND.

AFTER NELO DEPLOYED THE CHAYKIN DRONES, EVEN THE SMALL CREWS BECAME UNNECESSARY... THE PLOT LESS IMPORTANT.

THE BUSTLE ON NEW ATLANTIS... A HYPERMODERN POL EMERGING FROM THE OCEAN... BECAME SUFFICIENTLY CAPTIVATING... IT WAS A NEW SOCIETY NOT SEEN ON THE PLANET IN MILLENIA.

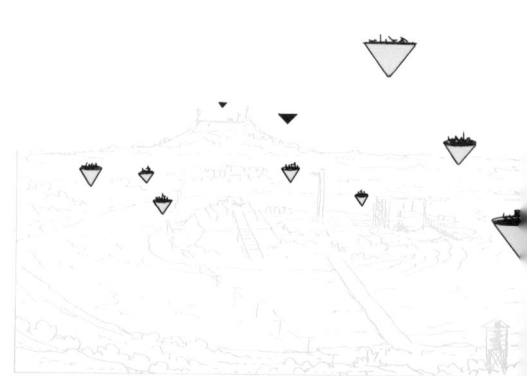

I DON'T KNOW HOW MY PRESENCE CONTRIBUTES

BUT I KNEW I DIDN'T WANT IT TO END

I CAN FIGHT AND BUILD MUSCLE... AND ACT WITH SINCERITY

I'VE DONE MANY FILMS AND SHOWS... BUT NONE WHERE I WANTED TO LIVE

HERE THE SCRIPT AND LIFE MERGED INTO ONE

MY SCRIPT IS MY CONSTITUTION I AM READY TO SMILE FOR ATLANTIS

E SHOW KEPT EVOLVING. A PREQUEL S PROPOSED ABOUT VIKINGS SAILING THE SOUTH PACIFIC.

BUT WHAT THE AUDIENCE CRAVED MOST WAS A SENSE OF UNCANNY FAMILIARITY. THEY SAW A VERSION OF THEMSELVES...

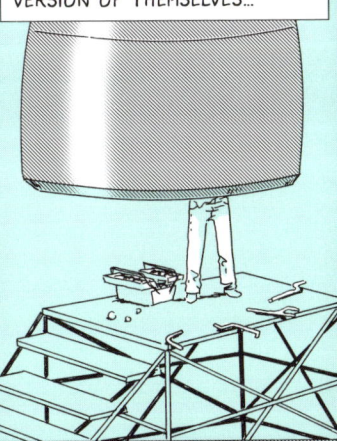

... WITH THE SAME JOBS... WITH A CRUCIAL DIFFERENCE: THEY DIDN'T WORK TO PAY MORTGAGES, BILLS OR CREDIT CARDS, THEY WORKED FOR A UNITED PURPOSE...

COLLECTIVE MISSION BEYOND EIR OWN MATERIAL NEEDS

HYPERFOCUSED ON ONE GOAL.

WHAT'S STATUS OF THE KIRBY ENGINE?

NOMINAL

CONQUEST OF MARS

WE DIDN'T KNOW IT AT THE TIME, BUT A NEW CIVILIZATION WAS EMERGING...

I WAS READY. WE WERE READY.

THIS ATLANTIS WILL NOT SINK BELOW THE SURFACE OF THE OCEAN.

WE WILL CREATE NEW OCEANS ON MARS.

I AM READY TO PLAY MY PART.

THE WORLD ALREADY FOLLOWS OUR EVERY STEP.

THEY WILL SUBMIT.

150 KM

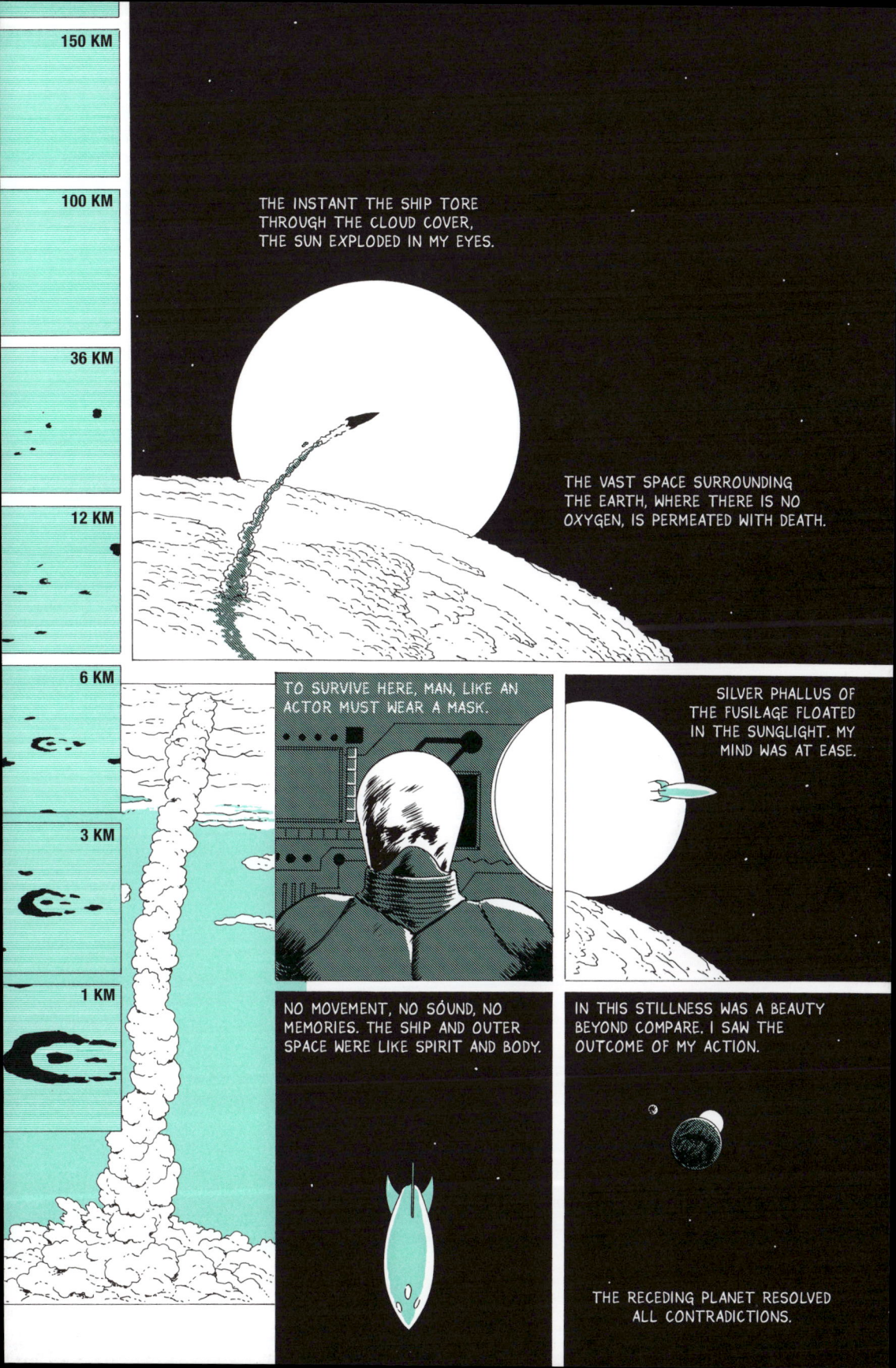

100 KM

THE INSTANT THE SHIP TORE THROUGH THE CLOUD COVER, THE SUN EXPLODED IN MY EYES.

36 KM

12 KM

THE VAST SPACE SURROUNDING THE EARTH, WHERE THERE IS NO OXYGEN, IS PERMEATED WITH DEATH.

6 KM

TO SURVIVE HERE, MAN, LIKE AN ACTOR MUST WEAR A MASK.

SILVER PHALLUS OF THE FUSILAGE FLOATED IN THE SUNLIGHT. MY MIND WAS AT EASE.

3 KM

1 KM

NO MOVEMENT, NO SOUND, NO MEMORIES. THE SHIP AND OUTER SPACE WERE LIKE SPIRIT AND BODY.

IN THIS STILLNESS WAS A BEAUTY BEYOND COMPARE. I SAW THE OUTCOME OF MY ACTION.

THE RECEDING PLANET RESOLVED ALL CONTRADICTIONS.

NOTES AND THEORIES*

Written and compiled by Adalbert Arcane

*Do not peruse whilst reading the comics

100,000 MILES

The author claims personal events inspired this story. The details are sketchy, but some information can be pieced together from various infrequent interviews. The author did live in the Washington, DC area at the time of the creation of this story. He claims his commute to his job (when he was employed on a secret prototyping division of AOL/TimeWarner (AOL/TW) headquartered near the Dulles airport) was approximately 45 minutes each way. This is plausible as traffic in the DC/Virginia tech corridor is notorious.

The imagery of the comic resembles the freeway edgelands of the Herndon/Reston/Sterling suburban sprawl one would have to traverse to reach the AOL/TW HQ.

J.G. Ballard's car novels influenced 100,000 Miles. The author makes this explicit on the page (see p. 14, panel 1). This author wears his influences on the sleeve.

This story distinctly breaks with the author's other work (collected as Trans Terra, which attempts a sharp social critique in comics form) both formally and narratively. The Beta Testing The Apocalypse (BTTA) project seeds already appear here: obsession with numbered titles, easter eggs that connect each story, sly references to the source material, absurd fictional scenarios, etc.

At what point is the traffic jam real, a real object, an entity that has existential status? The author complicates the ontological status of the traffic jam. Sometimes we drive, and traffic seems to flow without delays, but another traffic jam is already forming somewhere ahead of us. Is each traffic jam a distinct entity? Or is the entirety of the automobile fleet simply in various states of the same continuous global traffic jam in various states of territorialization and deterritorialization? These ideas parallel Timothy Morton's work on hyperobjects and the contemporaneous work of the Object-Oriented Philosophical clique. OOP proposes novel metaphysics, reevaluates the ontological status of objects, and posits a positive flat ontology (more on this in Million Year Boom below).

The now-famous denouement of the infinite traffic jam sets the stage for the ongoing questioning of the ontological status of everyday reality throughout the book. This sequence is likely the genesis of the whole BTTA project.

10,000 YEARS

On the surface, 10,000 Years resembles classics of science fiction like HG Wells' The Sleeper Awakes, or Edward Bellamy's utopian magnum opus, Looking Backward. It follows the familiar trope of a sleeping man, who, through some unexplained time fluke, awakens in the future. In most variants of this trope, the future is something concrete. It is something we fear or desire. The future tends to be either positive or negative, utopia or dystopia.

The one thing our modern imaginations cannot fathom is a future that is fundamentally the same. And yet, this was the state of humanity for millennia. Imagine a caveman troglodyte living during the paleolithic 40-50 thousand years ago. Was there a future for such a man? Did he imagine a world of tomorrow? Was he filled with imagined new Neolithic technologies? It is doubtful (and yet it DID happen at some point in time. How? When? See Music For Neanderthals). And yet, this is precisely how we imagine the future: an exponential improvement or absolute disaster, a catastrophe, an apocalypse. No one imagines the present extending infinitely into the future. The eternal present is the provenance of animals, not humans.

This story is remarkable for being written and published years before Peter Thiel's Zero To One business screed. In this book, Thiel (has Thiel read this comic?) posits that the economic development of atoms (machines, devices, physical items) has not kept up with the growth of bits (programmatic computer products, VR, big data, etc.). The power and speed of computers have increased, but in the physical realm, we have not made much progress. Much of the world exists on the infrastructure invented, built, and developed in the 20th century. 10,000 Years is a concise and prophetic elaboration of Fukuyama's End of History thesis. We are forever suspended in this world like a dead fetus floating in embalming fluid unless something or someone can get us out.

In the final sequence, the protagonist learns that he is a Martian or potentially Martian. It represents the author's intuitive understanding that the current static consensus can only be shaken loose by something external (to capitalism, civilization, humanity, and the planet).

The vision of Marxist zombies on Mars is a literal nod to the specter that has haunted history: Marx and Marxism and progress itself. The external event alluded to is the colonization of Mars (see Utopia Dividend) which (in theory) would accelerate (note: this is distinct from accelerationism) technological development in the material sphere, exploit vast new energy sources, and generate a vast quantity of new economic opportunities in the off-world colonies (see Blade Runner).

Zombie Marx's detourned speech, "A specter is haunting Mars – the specter of consumerism. [...] Consumers of the solar system, save your receipts." It is a haunting passage that both reaffirms that the proletariat is dead – subsumed by the consumer-tariat – and points towards the current form of late-socialist activism: specifically, the "I've got the receipts" brand of cancel culture that haunts social(ist) media.

100 DECIBELS

It is currently unknown why the author has created this comic. It is also clear that he had not read Schopenhauer's On Noise at this time.

976 SQ. FT.

Another story which the author claims is autobiographical. We have been able to corroborate some of the details. For example, the map (p. 36) included with the story is accurate, the area depicted exists in Brooklyn, just around the Manhattan Bridge overpass. Apocryphally it appears that the small neighborhood near DUMBO (Down Under the Manhattan Bridge Overpass) and Vinegar Hill, briefly attempted to rebrand as RAMBO (Right After the Manhattan Bridge Overpass). The move was spearheaded during the irrational years in the run up to the bursting of the real estate bubble and the inauguration of a major recession of the American economy (Global Crisis of 2007-8). We can confirm that several massive condominium complexes were being built in and around the neighborhood at the time, so the psychological effects of the structure are plausible.

The story is ostensibly a gentrification horror story. It is a trope common enough and not particularly original. Typically, a new construction disturbs the residents of a neighborhood. The mystery is solved when the source of the haunting is a disturbed grave, burial ground, or some other source of crime that stains this piece of land (see Poltergeist, Pet Semantary, etc.). However, this story subverts the trope by placing the source of the haunting into the future.

Why should only the past haunt us? Why can't the future, haunt us as well? This is a properly Hauntological horror story.

We can also confirm that an old woman named Nadine lived in the area and she owned a small dog.

WHITE NOISE

At the time of creating this story, the author claims he was not aware of Don DeLillo's novel with the same title (see Hotel Silencio and Noise, a History).

PHASE TRANSITION

"Walter Gropius published photographs of Buffalo's grain elevators in the Jahrbuch des Deutschen Werkbundes (Yearbook of the German Association of Craftsmen) in 1913 (the same year Marcel Duchamp made the first of his many Bicycle Wheels)." Ten years later, in Vers une architecture, Le Corbusier called grain silos "the first fruits of the New Age."[1] Now, almost 100 years after the inauguration of modernist architecture, we live in the civilizational equivalent of an orchard strewn with rotting fruit.

When one first encounters a silo there's a feeling of uncanny familiarity. The shape and the presence of the structure is like encountering a primal form, a template[2+3] for the world we encounter today; a beautiful functional form, but hollow, drained of its original functionalist context.

NOISE, A HISTORY

Noise, a History was written and drawn before

Music for Neanderthals

Music for Neanderthals. This one page distills the author's interest in the development of sound, noise, and other auditory phenomena. One can imagine the Big Bang, the silent explosion of our universe into being, as containing all the sounds of the universe. Think of white light comprising all the colors of the visible and invisible spectrum. When you add all the sounds together, do you get silence? Or a massive cacophony? We are constantly detecting sounds produced by that ur-explosion. The history of civilization is discovering and manufacturing new auditory phenomena and the privatization of sound.

MILLION YEAR BOOM

Million Year Boom, the best-known story by the author, found its way into the celebrated Best Nonrequired Reading anthology. It's another Ballard-influenced story that excavates the primitive drives concealed within us under a thin veneer of civilization.

We demand a greener future. Global warming is irrevocably changing the planet. Humanity has become a geological agent, like asteroids, tectonic shifts, or bat guano. Our civilization will leave a marker on geological strata. "This is the Anthropocene! We are the gods of destruction. We must do something!" At least that's what we like to tell ourselves.

Our late-capitalist societies (late for what?) should account for all undervalued externalities (think greenhouse emissions, or exporting waste, etc.) in our biosphere. Imagine this scenario pushed into the absolute limit. Under this new regime, the entire biomass of the planet would have to be counted, weighed, measured, understood, and monetized. This kind of hyper-rationalization of all matter and biomass on the earth would result in a new scientific techno-animism.

Science and big tech do not create knowledge but clouds of data. We see science and data as a solution, but we should view it as another kind of pollution, a destabilizing process that deter-

---

1 What Modernism Learned from the World's First Grain Elevator By Jennifer Kabat (https://www.frieze.com/article/what-modernism-learned-worlds-first-grain-elevator)

2 The temple was the original template. The hidden source of Plato's eternal forms which he glimpsed during his initiation into the Eleusis Mysteries ("blessed sight and vision" witnessed in a "state of perfection"[3]).

3 Murarescu, Brian, The Immortality Key, p. 24

ritorializes societies. It is a paradox that most scientists and intellectuals have not grasped. Cyclical theories of development grasp this intuitively. Agrarian societies think in terms of growing cycles:

- spring > summer > fall > winter

Cosmopolitan societies (Greece, Rome, Medieval Europe, etc.[4]) think in terms of great ages:

- golden age > bronze age > decadent age > the fall

These modes are analogous. Our modern society, on the other hand, thinks in terms of eschatological teleology:

- present > gap of time > utopia or dystopia.

In other words, the future is binary (good/bad), and it exists at an unknown distance from us. The critical difference is that we do not view ourselves as human (animal) anymore. Since we broke the cycle, we now see ourselves as beyond nature. Even all the green activists view the planet as something to protect (we are more significant than nature) or insist that we must de-industrialize (i.e., to devolve, implicit in that demand is our already existing evolution beyond nature). There is no understanding of the forces that we unleashed in this paradigm.

To continue as a species, we need to understand two things: the cycles of a planetary society and who we are.

There is no one cycle, but there are two that matter above all:

- Art > Religion > Science > Magic
- Conquest > Consolidation

We are animals who master territory.

....

4   Please note that I am primarily concerned with western cyclical notions. The work as a whole is a commentary in the decline of the west.

The valuation of all capitalist externalities is analogous to the valuation of attention (screen time, participation, engagement, and other such metrics). However, we must supplement this process of material valuation with a spiritual (mental, ethereal) valuation. Nietzsche was trying to convey this with his reevaluation of all values notion in *Genealogy of Morality*. Marx's theory of value makes similar claims.

These revaluations will happen whether we like them or not, so we must do so in a controlled fashion.

The future is a choice between two options: option one, global society will become destabilized and (d)evolve into a kind of techno-cyber-animist magic niche-cults that compete for the scarce planetary resources. The other option is harnessing off-planet resources. In other words, to continue our unstable but productive expansionary economics, we must expand our energy inputs using extra-planetary resources (see Utopia Dividend).

If every blade of grass has monetary value, how is that different from the animistic kami of Shinto religions? Already we can see the sprouting of this ideology in the green movements. The recent rumored correspondence between Greta Thunberg and infamous eco-terrorist Ted Kaczynski (no relation to the author as far as we can ascertain) is but one of the many signs.

Economics and religious sentiments must not mix. The economic sphere must remain autonomous and independent. We must take steps to forcefully bracket economic activity from intersecting with spiritual matters. The mixing eventually results in for-profit religions, magic, and art. The blending is productive and exciting but also destabilizing and debasing. Material valuation of immaterial spheres is a recipe for disaster. These spheres should remain independent.

Though we would be loath to admit it, Marx attempted a Nietzschean revaluation of capitalist values into communist or socialist ones. Unfortunately, his critique smuggled religious, psychological, and magical values into economics. His famous formulation: "All that is solid melts into the air," is the equivalent of let there be light or god's breath that animated dead clay. If Marx flipped Hegel right side up, then we must do the same with Marx.

The Base > Superstructure formulation is another pyramid scheme. These formulations are clarifying in the same way that a pyramid explains the power relations embedded in society. By naming the devil (Capital), Marx gave it power unimagined before.

The subsequent invention of Marxist analysis and critical theory by the Soviet states and the Frankfurt school is almost algorithmic:

- Input: critique of the power of capital
- Output: capital increases its power

It will always invent a new way for Capital to win.

Critique is an incantation and invocation. For a similar example, see Foucault's life work (for example, on the discursive construction of sexuality in the 19th century). Words are the key to postmodern critique; it relies almost entirely on verbal games. These are a form of magic. The theorists are under the impression that they are banishing the entities they describe. Instead, they give them more power by concretizing them, naming them, and materializing them out of a previously fluid notion. Many demons are born in theory courses.

The dénouement of the story (p. 69-70), the awkward conflagration between Segway-riding (remember the Segway?) security guards and amped-up business execs, and the resulting bloody sigil are a prophetic sign of things to come.

The valuation of all matter is flat metaphysics (flat ontology), where all objects (biotic or abiotic or virtual) exist at a single value status. These kinds of flat systems often carry with them holistic primitive valuations like ritual sacrifices.

For example, a society can achieve balance only by sacrificing entities (humans, animals, etc.). The value of each entity is equivalent in some way to the perceived value lost or gained. Hierarchical modern and proto-modern societies paradoxically lack these mechanisms. They do value some entities over others. But, the value of entities at the top emerges from the collective value of entities below. In other words, value flows up (in contrast to trickle-down economics, another name for socialism) and aggregates. These systems are unstable but very productive. Generating higher hierarchical levels (CEOs, Popes, politicians) can only be accomplished by raising the aggregate entities below. The system can improve through increased instability; this is the paradox of Capitalism. Only a continuously increasing energy input can temporarily stabilize it until the next growth crisis (see Utopia Dividend, 36th Chamber of Commerce).

COZY APOCALYPSE

This is the state of the world. We indulge in apocalyptic scenarios like candy. We see the movies, we read the books, we watch the news. "The apocalypse is around the corner! How awful! Why won't somebody *do* something!? Wouldn't our lives be more exciting if it really happened?" we wonder performatively on social media from our cozy couches.

HOTEL SILENCIO

"In the absence of sound, you become the sound."[5]

The quietest room in the world is in Minnesota, approximately five minutes from where the author currently lives. The story was written before the author moved into the area. It is unknown if he moved to be closer to the anechoic chamber.

The experience inside the chamber is described

....

5 https://www.atlasobscura.com/places/orfield-labs-quiet-chamber

as maddening. It is surprising how much humans rely on principles of echolocation for their stability and their relationship to the world. If memories are spatial as has recently been discovered,[6] then our selves—built from accrued layers of spatially tagged memories (we are a memory palace)—exist in a personal echo chamber that is constantly dependent on outside sound to orient itself (on the principle of echolocation).

The ambient sound of the world (see White Noise) acts as an aetheric substance that allows us to literally move through the world by orienting via sound and vision. It allows us to be outward-oriented, following the sounds and sights of the world or the desiring machine. This is also known as a 'body without organs' in Deleuzian terms.

When you 'become the sound' inside the anechoic chamber, that relationship is fundamentally broken. The sound of your own organs reminds you that there's no there, there. There's nothing to anchor you to the outside. The phone call (of your consciousness) is coming from inside the house! The desiring machine breaks down. You become 'organ without body'… analogous to a schizophrenic steaming mass of microbial life arranged in shapes and patterns chattering miasmic fluid viscous semi-liquid bag of mostly water skin stretched tight like a drum. Who is playing the drum?

MUSIC FOR NEANDERTHALS

Who invented the future?

Music For Neanderthals is the culmination of the author's exploration of sound, started in the short one-page strips peppered throughout this collection (100 Decibels, White Noise, Hotel Silencio, Noise: A History). Did the Neanderthals sing? We don't know for sure. A better question might be, what did they hear?

....

6   "Your Mind is a Vast Landscape" by Adalbert Arcane in *Cartoon Dialectics* #2, Uncivilized Books, 2020.

The nascent field of archaeo-acoustics has been bringing to light some interesting findings. We know, for example, that Neanderthals made musical instruments. The famous Neanderthal bone flute of the Divje Babe grotto made out of a femur of a cave bear is just one example. The eerie sound of the flute (a replica was produced and performed by Ljuben Dimkaroski) as performed in a variety of cave settings proved that our ancient ancestors valued acoustics as much as simple shelter[7].

Why did the Neanderthals die out? Did modern humans (homo sapiens) bring about their demise along with the megafauna upon which they hunted? One rogue archaeologist posits that there was a kind of species war that our ancestors engaged in. The 'musical' instruments of modern humans have been discovered to produce sounds that drive certain animals mad. One hypothesis proposes that Neanderthals had a higher audible range than humans. Some unusual Aurignacian bone flutes date to a time when both Neanderthal and humans occupied the area. The flutes would've produced sounds beyond the range of human hearing but would've been audible to Neanderthals. Deployed at volume in an acoustically significant cavity, the sounds would've amplified to a pitch that drives many animals into a blind rage. Would Neanderthals have been affected similarly? Are we just now unearthing the deep history of cross-species acoustic warfare?

THE NEW

What is 'new'? What is 'old'? Much of our civilization is built on the pursuit of novelty. Our species abandoned the near-constant din of nature by creating and occupying cities. Inside cities, we have attempted to reconstruct the vibrant productivity characteristic of tropical ecological zones (for example, tropical rainforest). High productivity and availability of resources (food,

....

7   Most caves that have been inhabited for long time (and this is *deep* time, many caves were continuously inhabited for tens of thousands of years… imagine anything of our modern civilization lasting that long) are also acoustically significant.

water) create intense Darwinian competition for resources among various species. However, what results is not what is usually called "survival of the fittest" (i.e., one who is the strongest) but the "survival of the fitting-est," or one who fits best (as in fitting in a box).

High production zones are characterized by the multiplication of ecological micro-niches. There is intense competition to occupy a specific niche, but if your species can specialize into a sub-niche, the competition lessens, and the species becomes master of the niche. A massive multiplication of niches in high productivity zones looks like… a tropical rain forest. It is characterized not only by a multiplicity of species but also by a multiplicity of ecological niches.

This creation of niches is the key to novelty. Each niche (as long as it is ecologically viable) will produce a new species to occupy it. If you have many niches, you will have many species and subspecies. This is the hidden logic of Darwin's evolution. The biggest mistake for Darwin is the use of the word 'survival.' It has created countless misunderstandings. Species do not seek to survive. They seek to master and occupy their territory. The territory has a double meaning; territory as a specific area of land (or sky) and territory as an ecological niche. I would like to coin the term *terratory* to express this double meaning. On individual (or tribal, herd, flock) terms, we speak of land. On species terms, we speak of niche. The two are related. A niche cannot exist without territorial boundaries; therefore, the value of physical territory (for an individual or species) is only valuable if it exists within the boundaries of the ecological niche[8].

Mark Fischer lamented the end of *the new*. He thought that digital technology has devolved all culture into a nostalgia culture. All genres and all music (and other cultural artifacts) are now readily available via technological means. We cannot invent anything new anymore. The horizon is closed. We can only regurgitate and recycle the old into a kind of simulacrum of the new. We entomb the things that gave us joy in the past within the cultural specificity of the present. In the process, we drain (vampire-like) all the vitality that brought it into being. We mine the past for treasure to bring about a simulacrum of the new. Maybe there is an obscure old thing no one has seen? That is the quintessence of 'the new' as it is formulated today. It is really just 'neow' (neo-new, pronounced like 'meow'). The prefix 'neo' now needs to be affixed to 'new' to identify this process.

To create a proper 'new,' we need a new niche. Humans are one of the only species that have been able to leave their native niche (which they occupied as aquatic primates on flooded savannahs of Africa) and terraform whatever new ecological niche they encounter into one that is habitable. What kind of animal are we? Many posit that we are tool users, thinkers, players, etc. But humans are a kind of meta-species, the first species that can create their own niche, a terraforming species.

---

productivity and money) and you have the formula for the generation and multiplication of musical genre niches. The first mutation was hip-hop (Kraftwerk + vinyl sampling + rap vocals (i.e., poetry)… see pioneering tracks like Afrikaa Bambataa's "Planet Rock"). It was a potent formula which instantly generated many sub-genres (electro, post-punk, industrial, house, techno, big beat, etc.). The global economy which included post-colonial client states also created the perfect opportunity for sample hunting on the edges of the western economic sphere. Exotic musical styles, tribal rhythms, native instrumentation, indigenous music scenes, were rapidly absorbed and mutated into new styles (dub, trip hop, chillout, world, trance, jungle, etc.). By the time we enter the '90s, electronic music achieves a kind of autonomy from its ancestors and becomes a specific species with sub-species. (IDM, Electronica, EDM, etc.) By the beginning of the 21st century it has grown its own labyrinthine ecosystems (dubstep, grime, twostep, etc.). Each genre occupying specific niches which often correspond to specific economic and cultural epiphenomena.

---

8   This logic extends to the cultural activities of humans. Take as an example, the multiplication of genres in electronic music over three decades ('80s, '90s, '00s). Electronic music began as a sub-genre of rock and roll. The Krautrock band Kraftwerk laid the basic foundations and contours while using expensive analog electronic instrumentation. By the '70s and '80s, technology and economic productivity created the twin pillars of future electronic music: cheap digital technology (for synthesis and sampling) and massive ubiquity of cheap vinyl records (doubled as sample library and as an instrument itself). Pair this development with high economic growth (i.e.,

We have terraformed Earth already. As with all species that succeed in their niche, dangers await. These can be listed in the famous formulation devised by Donald Rumsfeld:

- known knowns (example: overpopulation: we know it is something that must be addressed)

- known unknowns (example: the destruction of the ecological niche: climate change or pollution, we know it's here, but we don't know the exact contours and extent)

- unknown unknowns (example: what else is coming? Singularity? Asteroid?)

Overpopulation is often 'fixed' by a mass die-off due to resource scarcity, and the population reverts to a new equilibrium point. Humans have primarily solved this by implementing various marriage and family programs through religious or political edicts. The destruction of the niche often leads to the destruction of the species. However, because of the meta-status of humans, we are aware of all this. We understand (implicitly—known unknowns) that these dangers exist. The unknown unknowns are, by their nature… unknown. On top of that, there's a fourth danger which can be summed up as:

- unknown knowns

What are the capacities and knowledge that we already possess that can be used to avert a crisis? Or at least kick the can down the road for another few hundred years? When considering the human biosphere, we usually only discuss planet Earth. We are dimly aware that our tiny ball of wet dirt is a little piece of a vast interplanetary cosmos, but when we discuss the future of the human species, we only focus on the planet beneath our feet. But our planetary problems should put the dangers (and opportunities) beyond the Earth into sharp relief. We could do everything right on planet Earth. We could create a lush verdant utopian society with a perfectly balanced ecology… and we can still be wiped out by a single asteroid strike. We know this, but it is a kind of unknown known. As a species, we pretend it is not really an option. To prevent this scenario, we must take on the next challenge and do what humans do best: terraform the Earth… and other planets (see Utopia Dividend).

SKYWAY SLEEPLESS

Minneapolis is host to the most extensive skyway system in the world. It also contains the longest skyway in the world. The Skyway system was proposed in the early '60s by Leslie Park, a real estate developer, as a way for Downtown Minneapolis to compete with Southdale Center, the first enclosed shopping mall in America.

Southdale was built in 1956, by architect Victor Gruen, in Edina, a suburb of Minneapolis. It proved enormously popular and spawned countless copycat malls all around the globe. Early mall developments (including Southdale) were supposed to be part of a larger masterplan which also included living space and pedestrian access. Across the board, most of these plans were never realized, and malls became accessible only via massive parking lots that surrounded the building.

The popularity of malls accelerated suburban development and its consequence: the decline of city centers. The mallification of America pushed economic activity out of city centers and into the suburbs, triggering a country-wide city-crisis that culminated in New York's near-bankruptcy in 1975. Subsequent developments led to the mallification of city cores and their eventual revitalization through gentrification. As many modern professionals and creative class members began to return to cities, American malls began to decline. By 2007 no new malls were being built in the suburbs. It is telling that the first new mall built since then (City Creek Canter) is a mixed-use mini-city development embedded inside Salt Lake City downtown.

Many see the city and the periphery as competing zones. Architects and planners view the car-oriented suburbs as 'bad' and mass transit and pedestrian city cores as 'good.'

However, the COVID-19 crisis is beginning a potential second de-urbanization of America. Residents of dense central cores such as New York and San Francisco are fleeing into surrounding suburban spaces or neighboring underdeveloped states, escaping lockdowns and their could-be-infected neighbors. Continued uncertainty about the wisdom of high-density cities may yet vindicate the visions of early 20th-century suburban planners.

Gruen, a life-long activist for creating more pedestrian spaces, spent the rest of his life trying to atone for the suburban monster he helped unleash.

Southdale is the single most influential building in America. The introduction of enclosed shopping malls completely changed the urban structure of the country. We are still living with the reverberation and fallout of unfinished real estate development schemes from decades ago.

The Skyway system is also the subject of a popular song by The Replacements, a notable rock band.

The story should be read as a companion to *100,000 Miles*.

36ᵀᴴ CHAMBER OF COMMERCE

Never let a good crisis go to waste. The twin economic crises (the 2001 DotCom Bust (DCB) and 2007-8 Global Economic Crisis (GEC)) bookend the author's experience in New York City. The author arrived in NYC just before the DCB and left during the GEC (with a short excursion to the Elysian Car Parks of suburban Washington, DC). The DCB left an indelible mark on the author. The time and effort invested in the new internet economy evaporated overnight. Participation in the 'real' economy was shown to be fraught by the whims of an irrational market. Around this time, the author began to shift his effort back to comics after half a decade of near abandonment. You can say that was the decade of ressentiment against a country and its economic promises. A ressentiment based on the utopian and unfulfilled promises of a better, more prosperous world.

This is the time when the author conceptualized and created the *Trans*… tetralogy. *Trans Alaska*, *Trans Siberia*, *Trans Atlantis*, and *Trans Utopia*. The series can be characterized as an indictment on the very idea of Utopia, though it is disguised as an earnest search for one. It is unknown if the author was conscious of the narrative he was creating. Perhaps the discarded, and as of this writing unpublished, fifth chapter of the *Trans* series is a clue. The chapter veers wildly into a critical-magickal analysis instead of relying on more approved academic narratives. The chapter is rife with conspiracy theories, prophetic visions, and entrail readings. Its denouement an unfinished indictment of the very idea of human civilization. It is thought that during the gestation of this forbidden volume, the author created and conceptualized the idea for Uncivilized Books. The unprofitability of the market begat an unprofitable side hustle.

Crisis is impetus for change. You must change your life. The twin economic crises are still reverberating. The up-and-down waves of the market amplify and cancel out. Crises are our constant companions. Bronze Age Collapse, *Crisis on Infinite Earths*, Pandemics, Oil Crisis, Climate Crisis, ad infinitum. The next crisis is inevitable, but its shape, parameters, and extent are not apparent. Our economic systems and theories are inadequate to deal with this state of things. Capitalism is fundamentally optimistic. Anyone who starts a business from a lowly shopkeeper to a billionaire entrepreneur can attest to this. Everyone wants their business to make money. Even though we know as many companies are destroyed as are created, Capitalist ontology is fundamentally optimistic. Sticking to a Capitalist program is supposed to raise all boats. The underlying problems are often brushed away with statistical tricks and optimistic jingoism.

Communism, Socialism, and other Marxist variants are a much-needed correction. Marx introduced the idea of crisis into Capitalism. Even though he saw the many contradictions pervading Capitalisms, Marx (and all subsequent Marxists) introduced Christian moralism and eschatology into Capitalism. He rightly points to crises caused by internal contradictions. Still, Marx believes in a Final Crisis that will end Capitalism and phase shift the economy into some kind of unspecified Communism. But in the final analysis, Communism is Capitalism with Christian characteristics. As such, it functions purely as a critical force, a kind of *Reformation of Capital*. This aspect can be plainly seen in the development of ostensibly Communist systems of Eastern and Central Europe.

For Economics to become an actual science, it must borrow a page from geology and introduce catastrophism into its fold. Some forms of cozy-catastrophism are present in the theories of figures such as capitalists Joseph Schumpeter, Marxists like Marshal Berman or David Harvey. But in all those cases, they are either too optimistic (Schumpeter) or purely critical (the Marxists). For alternatives, we must look into deep antiquity and some unusual sidetracks. (see Utopia Dividend)

This story is the only work by the author translated into Portuguese.

UTOPIA DIVIDEND

Utopia, like happiness, is an emergent phenomenon. Planning, seeking, or optimizing for utopia as an end is not possible. The condition only emerges from the pursuit of mastery of terratory (see The New). Utopia can only exist as a proposal or a fleeting moment in the process of mastery. The mastery of terratory is not accomplished as individuals but as a species. There are many evolutionary steps to this goal:

- technological progress
- auto-domestication of the species
- production of ecological niches
- harnessing of energy

The idea of technological progress is well known and frequently discussed. This is what we typically think of when we think of human progress. I will not expand more on this topic at this time.

Auto-domestication of the human species is overlooked as a driving force in terratorial pursuit. To understand this concept, we must first become acquainted with the human *extended phenotype:* shelter.

Human subjects are thrown into the environment in which they live. There is always a mismatch between the environment (the niche) and the inhabitant. Humans evolved traits, abilities, and psychologies to conquer various ecological zones they are thrown into. There is a vast array of human diversity that has developed to inhabit a specific environmental zone. Humans achieve this by using their shelter-building abilities. Shelter and, by extension, cities are the extended phenotype of humans[9].

Because of the meta-ness of the human species, this shelter ability is expressed in many shapes and sizes. Humans (like hermit crabs) can either inhabit preexisting structures (trees, caves, abandoned ruins, islands, planets) or (like birds, beavers, moles) they can build their own structures (tents, burrows, sod houses, mud-brick buildings, stone temples, concrete cities). In some ecological niches, temporary shelters are better adapted than permanent settlements. In both cases, humans develop shelter strategies best suited to the environment.

The production of a surplus is another example

---

9 *Why Civilization Is Older Than We Thought* By Samo Burja (https://palladiummag.com/2021/05/17/why-civilization-is-older-than-we-thought/).

of the extended human phenotype. It does not simply emerge from market mechanisms as it is typically portrayed. It is important to remember that humans are pack animals. This always results in all pack-related labor being conceived and deployed with a surplus in mind. Excessive energy or effort must always be generated and expanded to enable intra-pack sharing and protect the pack against potential/inevitable future food/shelter shortages or spoilage. When building shelter, gathering, farming, etc., a surplus is baked into the activity. When an individual gathers only enough for himself, this is considered a failure. The idea of surplus production is deeply embedded in the human psyche and baked into the pack dynamics. It is also part of human physiology. We store excess calories as fat which can fuel our body during times of crisis when food may be scarce.

The shelter/human dynamic is autocatalytic and unbalanced. It is autocatalytic because, over time, it generates new humans that are better adapted to the shelter (terratory) than to the surrounding area outside their domain. Once a terratory is mastered through shelter, domestication (of other species), and cognitive mapping (of the territory), it becomes its own niche within a niche. The humans born in a conquered terratory are still primarily adapted to the previous version of the terratory (pre-terratorialization), and now they must adjust to this new sub-niche. This adaptation takes a variety of forms (tribes, clans, hordes, swarms, politics). As a sub-niche grows, it requires ever-expanding energy resources. This is what makes the human species unbalanced. Humans, like everything in the universe, are entropic. Creating new niches always cannibalizes energy resources from elsewhere. This instability is built into the very structure of our DNA. This is key to understanding how a utopian/green earth can be created.

There is only one way humans can turn Earth into Gaia, a "balanced" ecological system on the planet: utilizing off-planet resources. A few significant points need to be kept in mind:

- Deep time: earth ecology is a series of catastrophic cycles that have almost wiped out all life several times

- Deep space: whether we like it or not, we are a space-dwelling species already. Space surrounds us. We are in space. Many of the near-extinction events in deep time resulted from countless collisions with our cosmic neighbors, small or large.

- Off-planet energy: ALL energy used on the planet is already extra-terrestrial (solar).

- "Nature" thrives when humans are not present.

I will not spend much time on deep time and catastrophism. Several stories here hint at the infinite catastrophes bubbling under the surface of normality (see *White Noise*). Another good resource is *Cartoon Dialectics #2* ("Apocalypse, Extinction, Death, Eschatology" issue, published by Uncivilized Books).

Off-planet energy is relatively self-explanatory. Most of the biomass uses solar energy as a primary input to turn the raw minerals of the planet into bioavailable nutrients and building components. Even excavated energy (like oil) is stored solar energy.

It has been observed countless times that when humans abandon an area of the planet (due to natural catastrophe, civilizational collapse, nuclear accidents), nature rushes in and fills the void very quickly. For example, contrary to popular belief, much of the amazon tropical forest is an overgrown garden created and cultivated millennia ago by human civilizations. The existence, extent, and demise of these pre-Amazonian civilizations are still not well understood.

When environmental activists talk about isolating and preserving natural habitats, de-industrializing, and de-nuclearizing, they really speak about humans leaving the planet. This can be achieved through only two means: extinction or exodus.

I am going to assume extinction is non-negotiable (though possible). Exodus is the only viable way to go. Jack Kirby's classic unfinished masterpiece *New Gods* is an excellent example of the fates of humanity: New Genesis or Apokolips.

Darkseid's Apokolips is the fate of the planet if we abandon lofty goals. If we remain on the planet, we will become Morlocks. We'll excavate the Earth and turn it into a husk, a shell of its former self. Even if we don't get wiped out by a collision with an extra-terrestrial body, we will excavate the crater ourselves (see paragraph about autocatalytic), searching for Anti-Life.

New Genesis is the planet we desire. Note that New Gods' mega-city hovers above the planet. It is weightlessly raised above the surface. It allows most of the planet to remain in its natural state. Parts are used for crop cultivation, the rest a lush wilderness.

Compare The Source to Anti-Life as another revealing paradigm. New Genesis uses The Source for power which is extra-planetary energy. The virtuous (high-minded) nature of HighFather and the rest of the denizens of New Genesis allows them to make contact with power from beyond the planet. This frees the inhabitants to pursue higher goals and to become the best versions of themselves. Darkseid of Apokolips is obsessed with gaining control of Anti-Life. Anti-Life lies dormant within humans; it must be extracted and refined... like oil. The path of Darkseid is to subdue and squeeze populations to extract their power and to dominate them into submission to work, without complaint, in the satanic industries in the bowels of Apokolips.

Looking beyond and expanding outwards to fill the void of the universe preserves the soul of civilization and leads to New Genesis. Inward-looking pursuits that reject expansion and terratorialization lead into the empty and soulless hall of mirrors that lies at the lowest level of human existence and civilization as hell on Earth.

If we want utopia to emerge and live in New Genesis, Earth needs to become a Type II Kardashev civilization. The promised land and the kingdom of God await in the endless, eternal emptiness beyond the Karman line.

Soar into the void.

INDEX

20th Century, 24
   Limited, 53
21st Century, 26
36th Chamber of Shaolin, 151-152

Aboriginal, 60
Abstract, 10
Absurd, 21
Academic, 48
Acceleration, 11
Acne, 21
Acoustics, 38, 81
   Cave, 92-94
   Cosmic, 45
   Significant, 92
Advanced, 60
Advertising, 22, 147
   Ad(s), 21, 22
   Agency, 22
Aeon(s), 28
   New, 59
Aeron chair, 153-154
Afrikaa Bambataa, 176
Affordable Luxury, 40, 41
Aggressive, 25
Agony, 29
Agoraphobia, 48
Agriculture, 60
Air, 49
   All that is solid melts into, 24
   Conditioning, 12, 48, 64
   Space, 105
Airport, 57
Akashic Records, 21
Alchemy, 66, 126
Alien(s), 29, 35
   Bestiary, 28
Alienation, 25
All contradictions, 169
Allergy, 61-64
   Allergic Reaction, 60-70
Ambient, 86
American Flagg!, 166
Amino acid, 27, 66
Amniotic Fluid, 66
Anatomy is Destiny, 66
Ancient, 28
Anechoic chamber, 174-175
Animal, 50, 51, 65
Animism, 173
Antidote, 62, 75
Anti-life, 181
Anti-urban (see suburban)
Anthropocene, 172
AOL, 59-70, 170
Apartment, 26, 29, 31, 45, 58, 62, 63
Aphrodisiac, 77
Apocalypse, 16, 26, 72-78, 174, 180
Arcane, 50

Archaeology, 126
Archaic, 50
   Heritage, 61
Arcane, Adalbert, 170-181
Architecture, 9, 10, 11, 12, 13, 14, 22, 35-42, 101
   Anarchitect, 110, 134, 139
   Ancient, 98-99, 123-124
   Architect, 41, 98-129
   Architect-King, 140
   Cyclopean, 98, 123-124
   Delights, 110
   Drawing, 116
   Hidden, 16
   Model, 41, 99, 111, 116, 117
   Modern, 75-78
   School, 116
   Section drawing, 31
Art, 133-142
Artificial, 69
Asphalt, 15
Atlantis, 159-169
   New 159-169
Atmosphere, 29
Auto-
   catalysis, 180
   domestication, 179
Automata, 27
Automobile, 9-16, 25, 35, 36, 38, 39, 40, 42, 48, 49, 57-59, 63, 69, 76, 77, 81, 88, 89, 91
   Bus, 49
Avant-garde, 81, 111

Bacon, Francis, 163
Ballard, J.G., 14, 170, 172
BAP, 163
Baptism, 48
Bathysphere, 57
Beep (see Sound Effects)
Bellamy, Edward, 21-29, 170
Berman, Marshall 179
Big Bang, 53, 172
Billion, 27
Bio-currency, 61
Biodiversity, 67
Bio-economy, 61
Biofuels, 67
Biological compulsion, 27
Bioluminescence, 129
Biosphere, 61, 172, 176
   Complete Environment, 92
Blueprint, 15
Blood, 70, 105
Body, 27
Bohemians, 41
Book, 31
Boom, 54, 57, 67, 77, 109
   Resource, 126
Boredom, 62
Boring, 165
Bottomless, 57

Bourgeois, 41
   Skin, 64
Brand, 59, 64
   Branding, 164
   Experts, 59
   Team, 69
Broken,
   Nose, 87-91
   Teeth, 70
Bronze Age Collapse, 178
Brutal, 25
Bucolic, 14
Bull, 27
Bulletproof coffee, 150
Buoyancy, 29
Business, 57-70
   Card, 110
   Model, 69

Canine, 50, 51
Capital, 10, 174
   Global, 109
Capitalism, 174
   Late-capitalism, 172
   with Christian characteristcs, 179
Car (see automobile)
   Crash, 9, 10, 15
Carbon, 21
Cardiovascular System, 45
Carnivore, 27
Cartoon Dialectics, 175, 180
Casa Malaparte, 75-78
Cash, 25
Cat, 75, 76, 78, 124
Catastrophe, 126
Cave, 90-94
   As instrument, 92, 93
   Painting, 27, 65, 70, 92
Caveman, 27, 85-88,
Cayce, 21-29
Cellphone (see gadget)
Central Park, 53
Century, 26
CEO, 64, 69, 152, 165
Chaykin, Howard, 166, 168
Chemical, 62, 68
Chocolate Laxative, 22
Chronic Patient, 35
City, 9, 13, 14, 15, 16, 24, 98-129
   Acoustics, 87
   Ancient, 98, 123-124
   Big, 61
   Buried, 49
   Chandigarh, 110
   Constantinople, 53
   Dhaka, 99, 101
   Guangzhou, 99, 101
   Ho Chi Minh City, 78, 101
   Jakarta, 101, 111
   Lago, 101
   London, 111
   Mumbai, 99, 101

Nagasaki, 53
Nairobi, 101
of the Sun, 138
Oldest, 98-99, 123-124
Return to, 35-42
Rootless, 75
São Paulo, 101
Seoul, 99
Shanghai, 38
Speed, 101
Tokyo, 99
Uruk, 98-129
Walking, 110
Warsaw, 102
Civitas, 10
Civilization, 14, 25, 28, 45, 167, 180
    Antediluvian, 50
    Civilized, 48, 51, 126
    Civilizing, 58, 88
    Collapse of, 77
    Fetid, 51
    Domesticated, 48, 51, 67
    Proto-, 123
    Submerged, 57
    Trauma of, 51
Chaos, 24
Climate,
    Crisis, 178
    Cycles, 159
    Disaster, 67
    Micro, 60
Climax, 12
Clip-Art, 59
Cold-blooded, 27
Cold shower, 150
Collective, 14, 23, 38
    Disorder, 23
Colonialism, 165
Communication, 68
    Non-verbal, 70
    With inanimate objects, 98, 103, 123-125
Communism, 23, 24, 179
Communion, 27
Commute, 9-16, 35
Company, 59-70
    Apple, 67
    Ford, 67
    General Electric, 67
    IBM, 67
    Microsoft, 67
    Sony, 67
    Takeover, 69
Competition, 27
Complex, 60
Computer, 11, 22, 24, 26, 27, 39, 40, 59, 61, 63, 64, 65, 66, 69, 75, 77, 99, 109, 111
Conflict, 27
Concrete,
    Island, 36
    Manifestation, 77

Reef, 40
Sentinel, 49
Teeth, 39
Condominium, 23, 25, 36-42
    District, 26
Constipation, 69
Consumerism, 23
    Consumer, 24, 41
    Specter of, 23
    Preferences, 41
Consumption (see Shopping)
Control, 11, 25, 75
Corporation 152
    Corporate, 58-70
    Corporate Campus, 59-70
    Corporate Chieftains, 41
    Corporate Identity, 59-70
    Corporate kool-aid, 35
    Cthulhu, 67
    DNA, 69
    Global, 59, 70
    Housing, 58, 62, 63, 66, 68,
    Logo of the Next Great Global, 70
    Paleolithic, 27
Cosmopolitan, 59
Cosmos, 66
Creation, 14, 59, 61, 69
Creative Blockage (see Constipation)
Creativity, 61, 65, 67, 69
Credit, 24, 25
Crime, 134-142
Crisis on Infinite Earths, 178
Critique, 174
Cro-Magnon, 27
Cryptic, 57
Cubicle, 11, 24
Cul-de-sac, 14
Currency, 23,
Cycles, 173

Daily Routine, 49
Darkseid, 181
Darwin, Charles, 176
Darwinian, 100
Data, 103
Da Vinci, Leonardo, 152
Dead, 26, 126
    Living, 23, 24
Debt, 25
Decay, 50-51,
    Romance of, 77
Decibel(s), 31, 53
Deciduous, 60
Deconstruction, 16, 111
Deep Space, 53, 45, 180
Deep Time, 24, 45, 51, 53, 67, 70, 93, 98, 123, 128, 164, 175, 180
Defecation, 64
Defective, 35
DeLillo, Don, 172
Deluge, 51
Demographics, 36

Demographic Demons, 41
Demonic, 59
Density, 118
Deprivation Chamber, 11
Dérive, 110, 117
Descent, 57, 70, 75, 120
Designer Furniture, 40
Desire, 12, 25
Destroy, 123
Dimension, 38
    Inter-, 68
    Other-, 40
Disassembled, 16
Disaster
    Astral, 18
    Flood, 67, 76
    Earthquake, 123
Disco, 31
Disorder, 23
Dispassionate, 27
DJ, 21
DNA (see Genetic(s))
Dog (see Canine)
Downtown, 13, 36
Drained, 63
Dream(s), 22-25, 29, 37, 38, 87, 116-118
    Dreamer, 23
    Interpretation, 21
    Of revolution, 25
    Poliphylo, 110
Driver (See Individual), 16
Drowning World, The, 51
Drugs, 41, 62, 63, 64
Drunk, 21
Duchamp, Marcel 172
DUMBO, 36, 171
Dyphenhydramine, 41
Dystopia, 170

Eames,
    Lounge and Ottoman, 36, 39, 153-154
Earth, 27, 169, 177
    Back to planet, 85
    Terrestrial, 28
    Crust, 45
Echo, 87
Ecology, 60, 175-176, 180
    Ecological balance, 180
Economy, 61, 77
    Bubble, 100
    Economic Loss, 64
    Economic Value, 60
    Green, 65
Economics, 11
Effigy, 26
Egypt, 40, 50
Electro-magnetism, 29
Eleusis Mysteries, 172
Embalming, 124
Emergence, 23,

Empire, 165
End of History, 24, 171
End, the, 16
Energy, 67
    Battery, 105
    Dissipated, 102
    Nuclear, 49, 53
    Solar, 67
Entrepreneur, 27
Eon, 49
Epidemic, 42
Eruca Ingenium, 60
Eschatology, 16
Eternity, 11, 124
    Eternal Return, 24
    Eternal Sameness, 26
Evolution, 27, 66, 67, 69, 92
Exercise, 87, 149, 154, 163, 166
Exchange, 25
    Fluid, 70
    Genetic, 27
    Value, 61
Existential, 41
Exit, 12, 13, 14, 15
Experiment, 11, 78, 102
Explosion, 77
Extended Phenotype, 179
Extinction, 27, 60, 67, 180
Eye, 26, 69
    In the pyramid, (see pyramid)

Faith, 68
Fear, 16, 51
    Of Nature, 51
    Physiology of, 50
    Psychology of, 50
Feces, 64, 65, 69
Feral, 27, 48, 51, 100
Fertility,
    Cycles, 68
    Lawn, 75-78
Fertilizer, 69
Fetus, 28, 102
Financial, 11
Fire, 67, 77, 93
Fischer, Mark, 175
Flood (see Water)
Flora, 75-78
Folklore, 38
Force Field, 38
Forest, 60, 64
Foucault, Michel, 174
Foundations, 49
Freelance, 35, 148
Freud, Sigmund, 21, 25
    Psychic Freudian astrology, 25
Fukuyama, Francis, 171
Funerary Rites, 28
Future, 15, 65, 126, 134, 142, 175
    Abandoned, 102
    Engineering the, 65
    Futurism, 111

In retreat, 26
Uncertain, 15, 77

Gadget, 12, 22
    Cellphone, 22, 24, 25
Gaia, 180
Garbage, 26
Gastrointestinal Tract, 68
Genealogy of Morality, 173
Genetic(s),
    Corporate, 69
    Credit Crunch, 67
    Desire, 66
    DNA, 180
    Exchange, 27
    Genes, 93
    Genome, 28, 93
    Information, 27
    Martian, 28
Gentrification, 40
Geographical Amnesia, 42
Geometry, 40
    Sinister, 106
Giacometti, Alberto, 133
Girlfriend, 23, 26, 35-42
Global,
    Ambition, 59
    Bio-Currency, 61
    Finance, 99
    Warming, 76
Golf Course, 60
Graphic, 59
Gratitude, 149
Gravity, 29, 62
    Pressure of, 29
Greece, 173
Grimes, 165
Gropius, Walter, 172
Gruen, Victor, 177

Hacking, 41
Hammer, 23
Happening, 141
Harman, Graham, 112
Harvest, 69
Harvey, David, 179
Hashimoto's Disease, 42
Haussmann, Baron, 138
Haunt, 24, 28
Hedonic Treadmill, 13
Hegel, Georg Wilhelm Friedrich, 174
Helicopter, 100-102, 105, 106-107, 115
Heraclitus, 69
Hieroglyphics, 50
HighFather, 181
High Rise, 26, 38
Highway, 38
Hippie, 59, 64
History, 23
    End of, 49
    Historical Inevitability, 69
    Muscle, 88

Planetary, 61
Repeating, 126
Storm of, 23
Hollow
    Effigy, 26
Horizon, 49
Hotel, 81
Human(s), 13, 16, 45
    Feces, 64, 65
    Homo Sapiens, 93
    I-, 67
Humanity Melting Away, 29
Hummer, 38
Hunter-Gatherer, 67
Hypnotic, 88

Ice Age, 164
Illusion, 11
Imagination, 38
Imhotep, 40, 98, 122-127, 129
Immortality Key, The, 172
Immunity, 64
Inanimate Consciousness, 27
Incubator, 11
Independence, 11
Individual, 11, 14
Infantile, 25
Infection, 27, 61
Infernal Noise, 24
Infinity, 117
Information, 27
Infrastructure, 10
Insam Cha, 110
Insects, 45
Insomnia, 37, 39, 41
Instinct, 25
Insurrection, 77
Intelligence, 67
Internet, 36, 41, 59
    Website, 39
Interpretation of Dreams, 21
Invention, 67, 90
Investment, 69
Ipad, 76
IPhone, 67, 85, 87
IPO, 64
IPod, 53, 67

Jane Jacobs, 81
Jargon, 40
Job, 11, 22
Jobs, 147
Jungle, 78
Junk Mail, 36
    Psychic, 41
Junk Space, 41

Kaczynski, Ted, 173
Kardashev Type I, 169
Kardashev Type II, 181
Karman Line, 169
Kirby, Jack, 167, 181

Known knowns, 176
Known unknowns, 176
Kraftwerk, 176
Kung-Fu, 151, 154
Kutulu, 40

Labyrinth, 15, 41
Larynx, 85
Law,
    Enforcement, 78
Lawn care, 75-78
Leader, 23
Le Corbusier, 103, 110, 172
Lemuria, 161
Leviathan, 109
Library, 81
Liu, Gordon, 151-152
Logo, 9, 12, 21-23, 25, 36-39, 41, 42, 45, 48, 59, 64, 65-67, 69, 70
Lungs, 14
Lychee Cola, 22

Machine (or mechanical), 10,
    For Living, 58
    Mechanical, 27
Magnetic Fields, 117
Mall, The, 10, 12, 24
Maneval, Jean, 102
Map, 36
Market,
    Economics, 61
    High, 109
Marriage, 75-78
Mars, 21, 23, 24, 29, 167, 171
    Face on, 29
    Life on, 21
Martian
    Feel like a, 21
    I'm, 28
    Meteor, 27
Marx, Karl, 23, 24, 171, 173-174, 179
Marxism, 171, 174, 179
Meditation, 148, 163
Megalith, 98, 123, 124, 164, 167
Megalopolis, 11
Membrane, 15
Memory, 29, 64, 116
    Muscle, 13
    Spatial, 42
    Suppressed, 48
Meta-species, 179-180
Metropolis, 35, 58
Miami, 38
Million, 54, 57
    -aire, 38
Mimic, 27
Mineral, 27
Mirage, 50
Mirror, 15, 51, 93
    Reality, 15
Mishima, Yukio, 163, 169
Moai, 58, 62

Mobile, 22, 24, 25, 41, 76, 78, 87, 91, 94
    Structure, 110
Modern,
    Post-, 111
    Ultra-, 26, 58
    Womb, 66
Moment, 26
Monarch, 91
    Butterfly, 77
    King, 109, 112, 115, 127
Monitor, 22, 23, 26
Monolith, 23
Monster, 50
Morlocks, 181
Morphogenesis, 66
Morton, Timothy, 170
Multi-Tasking, 24
Mummy, 124
Murarescu, Brian, 172
Muscle, 13
Music, 53, 81, 85, 90, 91
    EDM, 176
    Electronica, 176
    IDM, 176
    Krautrock, 176
    Rock 'n Roll, 111
Musk, Elon, 151, 156-169
Mutant Flora, 38
Mutual Orientalism, 111
Muzak, 88
Mystery of Existence, 27
MySpace, 41
Mythology, 59, 123

Nagasaki (see City)
Native, 60, 75, 109
Nature, 180
Nausea, 28
Neanderthal(s), 27, 67, 82-94, 175
Negative, 13
Neighborhood, 26, 35-42, 118
Neolithic, 171
Neon, 13
Nervous, 16
New, The, 96-129,175-176
New Atlantis, 160-161, 163-164, 166, 168
New Genesis, 181
New Gods, 181
New York, 35-42, 53, 171, 177-178
Niemeyer, Oscar, 102
Nietzsche, Friedrich, 24, 173
Nightmare, 21-29, 37
Nile, 69
Noise, 85
    History, a, 53
    Pollution, 81
    White, 45
North America, 53, 67
Nostalgia, 13, 22,
Nuclear,
    Explosion, 53
    Power Plant, 49, 106

Nucleus, 75
Number, 24

Obsession, 62
Occasionalism, 112
Occult Force, 21
Occupation, 24,
Ocean, 38, 76, 158-159
    Oceanic, 57
    Of profit, 67
Odor, 65
    Scent of Destiny, 49
Office, 11, 21
    Cubicle, 11
    Park, 11
    Pyramid, 24
Oil,
    Crisis, 102, 178
    Minister, 110
    Reserves, 118
Ontology, 16
    Flat, 170, 174
OOP, 170
Opportunity, 64
Orbit, 28, 169
Organ(s), 45
    Without a Body, 175
Orgy, 12
Origin of Life, 27
Overpopulation, 177
Oxygen, 27

Paleolithic, 27, 67, 170
Panacea, 14
Pandemic, 178
Papier-Mache, 26
Paradigm Shift, 69
Paranoia, 39
Parking, 11, 12, 13, 24
    Lot, 11, 12, 13,
    Ramp, 13, 24, 59
Particle, 111
Pavlov, 86
Personal Audio Device, 53, 85, 90
Pet Semantary, 171
Phantom, 38
Phase, 46
Pheromones, 77
    Scent of Destiny, 49
Pizza, 61, 63
Planet
    Interplanetary, 23
    Wrong, 28
Planet Rock, 176
Plato, 172
Pleasure, 10
Poltergeist, 171
Pornography, 27
Post-Orgasm, 27
Prefab, 14, 39
Premonition, 86
Primal, 51

Primordial, 66
Private,
    Jet, 159-160
    Universe, 90
    Urination, 21, 68
Procrustes, 10
Projection, 61
Progress, 22
Profit, 27, 67
    Cycles, 67
    Pure, 69
Project, 38, 69, 112, 118
    Abandoned, 111
Prophecy, 86
Protoplasm, 27
Psychogeography, 42
Psychology, 11, 37
    Bipolar Disorder, 42
    Münchausen Syndrome, 42
    Psychologist, 22
    Psychology Ward, 42
    Psychological Warfare, 37
Psychic, 21
    Therapy, 21
Public,
    Go, 59
    Urination, 39, 69
Pyramid(s), 21, 24-27, 50, 98, 99, 106, 124
    Eye in the, 21, 24, 25
    of Giza, 164

Quasar(s),
    Frequency of, 25

Rabbit, 77
Radiation
    Electro-magnetic, 29
Radio, 21, 25, 45
Rain, 51, 76
RAMBO (Right After the Manhattan Bridge Overpass), 36, 40, 171
Rapid Prototyping, 66
Reality, 16
    Edges of, 117
    New 16, 75
Rebirth, 22
Refund, 24, 28
Replacements, The, 178
Repression, 25, 50
Repressive De-sublimation, 69
Reptillian, 27, 48
Resident(s), 26
Restructuring, 69
Retroactive, 61
Revolution, 23, 102
    Zombie, 23, 24
Rhythm(ic)
    Everyday, 90
    Static, 25
Road, the, 12, 15
Roman concrete, 164

Rome, 173
Rooftop, 35
Routines, 148-152
Rumble (see sound effects)
Rumsfeld, Donald, 177
Rustic, 14

Sacrifice, 25, 124, 126
SAD (Seasonal Affective Disorder), 42
Santorini, 53
Savage, 65, 67
Scar Tissue, 42
Scatology, 64, 69
Schopenhauer, Arthur, 171
Schumpeter, Joseph, 179
Scream, 45, 86
Secret, 64
Security, 25, 69
Segway, 69, 174
Self-Made Man (see Individual)
Self-delusion (see Individual)
Seroquel, 42
Sex
Sexual
    Display, 63
    Instincts, 25
    Sublimation, 25
Shanghai (see City)
Shaolin, 151-152
Shinto, 173
Shit, 64
Shopping, 12, 15, 24,
    Centre, 12, 24,
    Cold-blooded, 27
Sicle, 23
Silence, 29, 81
    Silent Scream, 45
Silent panel, 16, 28, 31, 36, 49, 64, 70, 76,
Silo, 49-51, 102-103
Situationism, 110, 111
Six Shell Bubble House (see Jean Maneval)
Skinner Box, 11
Skull, 27
Skylab, 134, 142
Skyway, 133-142, 177-178
Sleep, 31
    Sleeper, 22, 23,
Slum, 99, 100, 105-108, 118, 126
Society, 25, 85
    Consumer, 24
    Futuristic, 23-24, 91
Soul, 25, 93
Sound, 93
Sound Effects
    Aaahh, 51
    Aaaah, 39
    Aaaahhhhhhachoo, 60, 61
    Ba Beep, 94
    Bang, 81, 114
    Beep, 24, 78, 135
    Beep Beep Beep, 135
    Boom, 77

    Boop, 76
    Bzzzzt, 153
    Chew, 63
    Clack, 45
    Clap, 67, 111
    Click, 61
    Crumble, 128
    Ding, 49
    Dum, 92, 93
    Eeeyahh, 86
    Eeeyow, 86
    Encore, 111
    Go girl, 111
    Grind, 45
    Gurgle, 81
    Ha Ha Ha, 138
    He He He, 138
    Hello, 91
    Hmph, 94
    Itch,
    Klack, 61, 63, 64
    Klang, 81
    Knock, 59
    Leader, 23
    Mlak, 85
    Ngggg, 31
    Ouf, 86, 112
    Pat, 60
    Plat, 36
    Plish, 58, 63
    Pshhh, 21, 39, 66
    Pssshh, 29
    Shhh, 138
    Shhhjhhhh, 37
    Scratch, 86
    Skritch, 49-50, 63
    Slam, 31, 68
    Sleeper, 23
    Snap, 135
    Snarl, 90
    Sniff, 61-64, 86
    Sputter, 48
    Squeeeek, 63
    Rumble, 31
    Tak, 42
    Tap, 64
    Thok, 128
    Throb, 115
    Thud, 69, 81
    Thwip, 22, 24
    Touch and slide, 85
    Vmmmmm, 63
    Wham, 31, 81
    Whhhrrrrr, 45, 75
    Whrrrr, 48
    Whrrk, 127
    Whoop, 108
    Woop, 111
    Yeah, 111
    Zzzzz, 45
Soundtrack, 67, 86
Source, The, 181

Space, 13, 21
    Mental, 41
    -Time Continuum, 28, 68
Spatial, 13
    Quality, 13
    Discontinuity, 15
Spectator, 62, 63
Specter, 24, 40
Starlink, 162, 165
Starship, 161, 162, 163, 165, 167, 168, 169
Start-up, 59
Static, 25
Stocks, 21
Stone, 98, 123-124
    Age, 85, 86, 93, 164, 167
    Circle, 60, 61, 64, 65,
Structures, 134, 140, 142, 179
Subconscious, 16, 39
Subject , 21
Sublime, 25
Sublimation, 25
Suburban, 12, 14
    Eden, 77
    Enterprise, 59
    Isolation, 62
    Suburbia, 35, 57-70, 75-78
Subway, 21, 53
Surface, 57
Surplus,
    Gravity, 29
    Molecular, 27
Supernova, 45
    Solar Holocaust, 45
Suspended Animation, 16
SUV (Suburban Utility Vehicle), 10
Swimming, 58, 62, 63, 66, 68
Symbolic Container, 61
Symphony of the City, 53
Symptom, 63
Synergy, 69
Synesthesia, 93

Tabacco, 11, 14, 15, 61, 89, 94
TARDIS, 38
Tatlin, 110
Team Building, 65
Technology, 22
Tectonics, 45
Tentacle, 59, 64, 66, 67
Terraforming, 177
Terratory, 176, 180
Territorial, 50
Tesla, 165
Thiel, Peter, 171
Third World, 101
Threshold, 50
Thunberg, Greta 173
Time, 21-29
    Temporal, 49
    Travel, 21-29, 49
Tomb(s), 24, 98, 124-129
    Burial, 28, 37

    Silence of, 24
Towards a New Architecture, 103
Tower, 38, 39, 40, 41
Toxic, 87
Traffic, 9, 10, 11, 15, 16, 38
    Jam 9, 10, 15, 16, 57
    Apocalypse, 16
    Flows, 38
Train, 53
    Tracks, 50
Trajectories, 118
Trance, 22, 40
Transformers, 12
Trans Alaska, 178
Trans Atlantis, 178
Trans Siberia, 178
Trans Utopia, 178
Trauma, 50
    Of Civilization, 51
Tree, 35, 36, 37, 60, 61, 65
    Huggers, 60
Trends, 118
Tsunami, 164
Tunnel, 119-121 129
Turkish, 53
TV, 23, 48, 62, 81

Uncivilized Books, 178
Underground, 37, 119
Unknown knowns, 177
Unknown unknowns, 177
Unnatural, 86
Untamed, 51
Urban,
    Grit, 40
    Fallout, 105
Urbit, 164
Urinal, 21, 68
Uruk (see Citie)
Utopia(n), 110, 156, 170, 179
    Denouement, 25
    Hermetic, 40
    Possibility of, 102
    Wish fulfillment, 25

Vaccum Tube, 25
Vanishing point, 142
Vehicle, 16
Versailles, 10
Vertigo, 28
Video games, 147
Virile, 27
Virtual, 11
Virus, 27
Viscous, 15
    Reality, 11
Vision, 67
Vitruvian Man, 152
Void, 13
Volcano, 27
    Kratatoa, 164
    Santorini, 53

Vomit, 39

Walking, 85, 87-89
Water, 29, 58, 62, 63, 66, 68
    Fall, 53
    Flood, 67, 76
    Fluid, 27
Weapons, 24
Wells, HG, 170
West, 102, 111
    Exhausted, 111
Wham (see Sound effects)
White, 45
Wild,
    Man, 64
    Re-, 60, 67
Wilderness,
    Estates, 58, 62, 63, 66, 68
    Return of, 64
Window(s), 23
    Skylight, 35, 41
Work, 11, 15
World, 28, 90
    Drowned in a tub, 29
    Lost, 110
    New, 77
    Rotting, 51

YouTube, 162

Zeitgeist, 48
Ziggurat, 161, 163-166, 168
Žižek, Slavoj, 22
Zizmor, Katherine, 21, 25, 28, 29
Zodiac, 28
Zombie(s), 23, 171

ABOUT THE AUTHOR

Tom Kaczynski is a cartoonist, writer, and publisher. The book you are holding was nominated for the Eisner Award and published in four languages. Tom is also the author of the award-nominated *Cartoon Dialectics* series, and the forthcoming *Trans Terra* graphic novel. His comics have appeared in countless international publications, including *A Batahlia*, *The Nib*, *Mome*, and many others. Tom K is the founder of *Uncivilized Books*, a boutique graphic novel publishing house. Since its inception, Uncivilized Books has published acclaimed and award winning comics and graphic novels by Gabrielle Bell, Noah Van Sciver, David B., Joann Sfar, Sophie Yanow, Craig Thompson, and many others. Tom is also the co-founder (with Adalbert Arcane) of *Omniversity*, a theoretical think tank dedicated to researching the comics medium and the nature of the multiverse. He lives in Minneapolis with his partner Nikki, two cats, and a dog.

THANK YOU!

Nikki Weispfenning, Jonathan Bennett, Gabrielle Bell, Jon Lewis, Karen Sneider, Michael Drivas, Zak Sally, Dan Wieken, Alex Holden, Vanessa Davis, Mike Dawson, Aaaron Renier, Dash Shaw, Frank Santoro, Eric Reynolds, Gary Groth, Annie Koyama, Kevin Huizenga, Jon Wright, Warren Park, Mehmet Bereket, Mach Arom (RIP), Joanna Kaczynski, Emilia Kaczynski, Damien Jay, Christopher Brown, Daniel Chmielewski.